Museum

A DRAMA

By Tina Howe

SAMUEL FRENCH, INC.
45 WEST 25TH STREET   NEW YORK 10010
7623 SUNSET BOULEVARD HOLLYWOOD 90046
LONDON   TORONTO

Joseph Papp

Presents

Museum

By
Tina Howe

Directed By
Max Stafford-Clark

Scenery By
Robert Yodice

Costumes By
Patricia McGourty

Lighting By
Jennifer Tipton

With

**Gerry Bamman   Joel Brooks   Larry Bryggman
Steven Gilborn   Robyn Goodman   Kathryn Grody
Jane Hallaren   Dan Hedaya   Calvin Jung
Kaiulani Lee   Karen Ludwig   Bruce McGill
Frederikke Meister   Lynn Milgrim
Jeffrey David Pomerantz   Jean-Pierre Stewart
Kathleen Tolan   Dianne Wiest**

Associate Producer
Bernard Gersten

A New York Shakespeare Festival Production

MUSEUM was initially presented at the Los Angeles
Actors' Theatre on April 29, 1976 by Ralph Waite, Artistic
Director. The production was directed by Dana Elcar and
Richard Jordan.

CAST
(in order of appearance)

THE GUARD .... *Larry Bryggman*
MICHAEL WALL, 1st photographer .... *Bruce McGill*
JEAN-CLAUDE .... *Jean-Pierre Stewart*
FRANÇOISE .... *Frederikke Meister*
ANNETTE FROEBEL, lost woman .... *Kaiulani Lee*
LIZ .... *Robyn Goodman*
CAROL .... *Kathryn Grody*
BLAKEY .... *Kathleen Tolan*
MR. HOLLINGSFORD, lost man .... *Gerry Bamman*
ELIZABETH SORROW, silent woman .... *Dianne Wiest*
PETER ZIFF, silent man .... *Dan Hedaya*
MR. SALT, man with recorded tour .... *Steven Gilborn*
MRS. SALT .... *Jane Hallaren*
MAGGIE SNOW, lost woman .... *Lynn Milgrim*
BOB LAMB .... *Jeffrey David Pomerantz*
WILL WILLARD .... *Joel Brooks*
FRED IZUMI, 2nd photographer .... *Calvin Jung*
MIRA ZADAL, inquiring woman .... *Robyn Goodman*
FIRST MAN IN PASSING .... *Gerry Bamman*
SECOND MAN IN PASSING .... *Jean-Pierre Stewart*
BARBARA CASTLE .... *Lynn Milgrim*
BARBARA ZIMMER .... *Karen Ludwig*
MR. GREGORY, man with loud recorded tour ....
                                      Jean-Pierre Stewart
CHLOE TRAPP, curator .... *Kaiulani Lee*
ADA BILDITSKY, curator's 1st guest ...... *Frederikke Meister*
GILDA NORRIS, sketcher .... *Kathryn Grody*
TINK SOLHEIM .... *Dianne Wiest*
KATE SIV, Tink's friend .... *Robyn Goodman*
BILL PLAID, curator's 2nd guest .... *Jeffrey David Pomerantz*
LILLIAN, 1st laughing lady .... *Frederikke Meister*
HARRIET, 2nd laughing lady .... *Lynn Milgrim*
MAY, 3rd laughing lady .... *Karen Ludwig*
GIORGIO .... *Gerry Bamman*
ZOE, his wife .... *Jane Hallaren*
JULIE JENKINS, 3rd photographer .... *Kathleen Tolan*
FIRST GUARD .... *Steven Gilborn*
SECOND GUARD .... *Dan Hedaya*
STEVE WILLIAMS .... *Joel Brooks*
AN ELDERLY COUPLE .... *Steven Gilborn, Karen Ludwig*

4

CHARACTERS

Fixed characters
 THE GUARD
 MICHAEL WALL
 FRED IZUMI

Changing characters in order of appearance

Men	Women
JEAN-CLAUDE	FRANÇOISE
MR. HOLLINGSFORD	ANNETTE FROEBEL
MR. SALT	CAROL
PETER ZIFF	LIZ
BOB LAMB	BLAKEY
WILL WILLARD	ELIZABETH SORROW
TWO MEN IN PASSING	MRS. SALT
MR. GREGORY	MAGGIE SNOW
BILL PLAID	MIRA ZADAL
GIORGIO	BARBARA ZIMMER
FIRST GUARD	BARBARA CASTLE
SECOND GUARD	CHLOE TRAPP
STEVE WILLIAMS	ADA BILDITSKY
MR. MOE	GILDA NORRIS
	TINK SOLHEIM
	KATE SIV
	LILLIAN
	HARRIET
	MAY
	ZOE
	JULIE JENKINS
	MRS. MOE

AUTHOR'S NOTE

It is my hope that any group wanting to present *Museum* use the large cast size as a challenge and not as a restriction. The play was written to serve the versatility of actors. It has been performed with a cast of 44, each actor playing one role, and it's been performed by 18 with the actors doubling and tripling in their roles. It would be possible, though strenuous, to stage the play with only a handful of actors. By the same token, an entire school or community could be pressed into action in a production designed to recreate the crush of modern day museum going. Hopefully the staging possibilities are limitless.

This was the breakdown of roles used in the New York Shakespeare Festival production of 1978:

Male
> The Guard, a fixed role
> Michael Wall, a fixed role
> Fred Izumi, a fixed role
> Jean-Claude, Second man in passing, Mr. Gregory
> Mr. Hollingsford, First man in passing, Giorgio
> Peter Ziff, Second Guard
> Mr. Salt, First Guard, Mr. Moe
> Bob Lamb, Bill Plaid
> Will Willard, Steve Williams

Female
> Francoise, Ada Bilditsky, Lillian
> Annette Froebel, Chloe Trapp
> Liz, Mira Zadal, Kate Siv
> Carol, Gilda Norris
> Blakey, Julie Jenkins
> Elizabeth Sorrow, Tink Solheim
> Mrs. Salt, Zoe
> Maggie Snow, Barbara Castle, Harriet
> Barbara Zimmer, May, Mrs. Moe

TIME: The present

SCENE:
A group show of three contemporary artists entitled, "The Broken Silence." It is held in a vast white room on the second floor of a major American museum. There are several benches to sit on and the windows look out on skyscrapers.

A listing of the artists and description of their work:

ZACHERY MOE
    Born, 1943, Fort Wayne, Indiana

    Four gigantic pure white canvases, all identical
    "Landscape I," 197 *
    Acrylic emulsion and wax on canvas
    On loan from the Sidney Rubin Gallery

    "Landscape II," 197
    Acrylic emulsion and wax on canvas
    On loan from the Sidney Rubin Gallery

    "Seascape VII," 197
    Acrylic emulsion and wax on canvas
    On loan from the Sidney Rubin Gallery

    "Starscape 19," 197
    Acrylic emulsion and wax on canvas
    On loan from the artist

Author's Note: In the New York Shakespeare Festival production, the 4th painting, "Starscape 19" was hung on the
4th, invisible wall so that anyone looking at it was in fact
looking into the audience.

* The dates of completion for the artworks should correspond
to the year of the play's production. As the years pass, the
dates of the artists' births will also have to be adjusted.

———————————

AGNES VAAG
    Born, 1954, St. Cloud, Minnesota

    Nine small, decorative and menacing constructions made
    of animal teeth, feathers, fur, claws, bone, shell, wings,
    horn, scales, sponge, and antannae.

    "Sacred Inquisition, Daylight Savings Time," 197
    On loan from the Minneapolis Institute of Fine Arts

    "When the Archangels Abandon Their Grace," 197
    On loan from the Minneapolis Institute of Fine Arts

    "Prometheus Singed," 197
    On loan from the Minneapolis Institute of Fine Arts

7

"Socratic Dialogue," 197
On loan from The Corcoran Gallery of Art

"The Temptation and Corruption of William Blake," 197
On loan from The Whitney Museum of American Art

"Abraxas," 197
On loan from the Whitney Museum of American Art

"Ode to Emily Dickenson," 197
On loan from the Rhode Island School of Design

"Metaphysics Revisited," 197
On loan from the private collection of Igmar Vaag

"The Holy Wars of Babylon Rage Through the Night," 197
On loan from the private collection of Igmar Vaag

Author's Note: The actual number of sculptures displayed can vary according to the style and size of the set. In the New York Shakespeare Festival production, only six were shown.

STEVE WILLIAMS
Born, 1936, Santa Rosa, California

A clothesline runs 25 feet across the room. On it hang five life-sized figures left out to dry with their clothes on. They are spookily realistic and come apart and can be put back together again.

The first figure is a businessman dressed in a pin striped suit. One of his shoes is missing

Second, a bride billowing in satin and veils

Third, a Mexican boy in a tee shirt

Fourth, a self-portrait of the artist wearing blue jeans and a plaid lumber jacket

Fifth, a naked Chinese woman with bound feet

A basket of round headed clothespins sits under the clothesline to one side

"Wet Dream Left Out to Dry," 197

Construction of rope, cloth, paper mache, wire, leather, wood, plaster, and fibre glass

On loan from the Los Angeles County Museum of Art

8

MUSEUM

The audience should be encouraged to walk through the exhibit before the play begins.

THE CURTAIN RISES: *It's the last day of the show several minutes before the museum opens. The gallery is in darkness, nothing happens, then far away sounds of footsteps, doors opening and closing.*

THE GUARD. (*Walks briskly into the room. Turns on the lights, first the Agnes Vaag's are illuminated with pinpricks of light, then the Moe's are revealed, and finally the Clothesline. As* THE GUARD *brings everything to life, a voice sounding something like a combination of God and a newcaster announces:*)

VOICE. Sandro Botticelli's priceless masterpiece, "The Birth of Venus" was attacked and virtually destroyed yesterday afternoon by a hooded man armed with a hand gun who opened fire on the painting while screaming, "Cursed is the ground for thy sake." Before he was finally overcome by three guards and numerous bystanders, the heavily built assailant pumped more than 18 bullets into the nude Venus figure, literally shooting her off the face of the canvas. The Acting Director of the Uffizi Gallery which houses the masterpiece, said in an interview last night that it was the most violent attack ever made against a Renaissance painting. Restoration will be impossible.

THE GUARD. (*Stores this information along with everything else he knows and begins his daily process*

9

of becoming watchful yet as unobtrusive as possible.
He rocks on his heels, sucks his breakfast out from
between his teeth, picks fuzz off his uniform, hoists up
his underwear, and then waits.)

MICHAEL WALL. (*Enters carrying an arsenal of*
photographic equipment including a camera attached
to a tripod. He looks around the room, finds the
Zachery Moe's, and sets his gear down in front of
"Landscape I." He walks up to it, then backs away,
walks up close again and then takes out his light
meter for a reading. He adjusts his camera and pre-
pares to shoot, all with enormous concentration,
energy, and flair. THE GUARD *is mesmerized by him.*
After several moments, WALL *poises his finger on the*
shutter release.)

THE GUARD. It's against museum regulations to
photograph the art works.

MICHAEL WALL. (*Whirling around, furious.*) You're
kidding!

THE GUARD. It's against museum regulations to
photograph the art works.

MICHAEL WALL. Thanks alot for waiting to tell me
until I was all set up . . .

THE GUARD. I'm surprised they even let you in with
all that stuff . . .

MICHAEL WALL. (*Shaking his head.*) Too much!

THE GUARD. The attendant downstairs is supposed
to see that all photographic equipment is left in the
check room. . . .

MICHAEL WALL. I don't believe this . . .

THE GUARD. . . . and that includes binoculars, tele-
scopes, folding . . .

MICHAEL WALL. You wait until I'm all set up, tripod
locked, camera attached, "f" stop set . . .

THE GUARD. I've seen the attendant downstairs refuse visitors admittance who were just carrying . . . film!

MICHAEL WALL. . . . AND WHEN ALL OF THAT IS DONE, THEN YOU TELL ME IT'S AGAINST MUSEUM REGULATIONS TO PHOTOGRAPH THE ART WORKS!

THE GUARD. And not just film either, but radios, tape-recorders, typewriters and sandwiches. . . .

MICHAEL WALL. Who do I see to get permission?

THE GUARD. I've seen the attendant downstairs stop visitors who had bulging pockets.

MICHAEL WALL. (*Detaching his camera from the tripod.*) The Head of Public Relations? The Administrative Assistant?

THE GUARD. The public has no respect for "place" anymore.

MICHAEL WALL. The Curator? The Chairman of the Board?

THE GUARD. They wear tennis shorts to church. They drink soda at the opera. They bring flash cameras to museums. . . .

MICHAEL WALL. (*His camera in hand, walks up to* THE GUARD *and starts snapping his picture.*) Come on, who do I see for permission to photograph the art works? (*Taking a picture with each guess.*) The Cinematic Representative? The Acting President of the Exhibition? The Liason for Public Information? (*Pause.*) You have an interesting profile.

THE GUARD. I've caught men exposing their genitals in this room!

MICHAEL WALL. (*Getting involved with* THE GUARD *as a model.*) Good cheek bones!

THE GUARD. Certain shows . . . inspire that!

MICHAEL WALL. . . . strong chin . . .

THE GUARD. 19th Century French Academy nudes encourage . . . flashing.

MICHAEL WALL. (*Adjusts* THE GUARD'S *head for a shot.*) Hold it . . .

THE GUARD. (*Voice lowered.*) You'd be surprised, the shortest men have the most swollen genitals . . .

MICHAEL WALL. Nice . . . nice . . .

THE GUARD. (*Flattered, shyly poses for him.*) And there don't even have to be women in the room in order for these . . . shorter men to expose their swollen genitals. . . .

MICHAEL WALL. (*Still snapping.*) Come on, give me a hint. Do I see the curatorial staff or the administrative staff?

THE GUARD. Very few women expose themselves.

MICHAEL WALL. (*Taking closeups.*) Nice, very nice. . . .

THE GUARD. Though I *have* seen a few younger women lift their skirts and drop their panties.

MICHAEL WALL. Please! Who do I see to get permission to photograph the art works? (THE GUARD *and* MICHAEL WALL *are still as.*)

JEAN-CLAUDE and FRANÇOISE. (*Enter, a French couple in their 30's. They are very serious museum goers. They advance to the Moe's.*)

JEAN-CLAUDE. (*Looks at "Landscape I", then consults his bilingual catalogue.*) Voici, Zachery Moe!

FRANÇOISE. Ah oui, Zachery Moe!

JEAN-CLAUDE. (*Reading from his catalogue.*) "Le publique qui s'intéresse a l'art est tenté de ne voir que chaos dans la profusion des tendances de la peinture contemporaine . . ."

FRANÇOISE. (*Looking at the painting.*) Il à un style . . . un style . . . tout à fait. . . .

JEAN-CLAUDE. "Trop près pour distinguer l'authen-

tique du factice, il est le témoin trop passionné de la
frénésie d'être divers qui est le propre des artistes de
notre temps. . . ."

FRANÇOISE. Tout à fait. . . . tou à fait . . . FRAG-
ILE!

JEAN-CLAUDE. "Il est troublé par la surproduction
de la matière peinte. C'est une des singularités les plus
cocasses de notre siècle. . . ."

FRANÇOISE. Mais viens voir, Jean-Claude! Regards
la peinture!

JEAN-CLAUDE. . . . "qui abonde pourtant en du-
peries de toutes sortes . . ."

FRANÇOISE. C'est une fragilité . . . mystique . . .
une fragilité . . . religeuse . . . une fragilité. . . .

JEAN-CLAUDE. (*Finally looks at the painting.*)
PLASTIQUE! Une fragilité plastique, Françoise!

FRANÇOISE. (*Disagreeing.*) Une fragilité . . . sym-
boliste!

JEAN-CLAUDE. Une fragilité . . . moderne!

FRANÇOISE. Une fragilité dix-septieme siecle!

JEAN-CLAUDE. Une fragilité psychologique!

FRANÇOISE. Une fragilité . . . fragile!

JEAN-CLAUDE. AH OUI, SURTOUT UNE FRA-
GILITÉ FRAGILE!

FRANÇOISE. C'est le mot juste. . . .

JEAN-CLAUDE. Fragile. . . .

FRANÇOISE. Un adjectif exact!

JEAN-CLAUDE. Comme . . . futilité *futile!*

FRANÇOISE. Ou . . . frivolité *frivole!*

JEAN-CLAUDE. Fraternité *fraternelle!*

FRANÇOISE. Ou même de la . . . folie *folle!*

JEAN-CLAUDE. (*Kissing her in appreciation.*) Françoise, je t'adore! (*They gaze up at "Landscape I."*)

THE GUARD. (*Softly to* MICHAEL WALL.) The Director!

MICHAEL WALL. What?

THE GUARD. The Director.

MICHAEL WALL. What about the Director?

THE GUARD. It's the Director who gives permission to photograph the art works!

MICHAEL WALL. (*Incredulous.*) THE DIRECTOR?

THE GUARD. The Director!

MICHAEL WALL. It just . . . never occurred to me that . . . the Director. . . .

THE GUARD. (*In unison, smiling.*) . . . the Director.

MICHAEL WALL. (*Amazed, gathers his equipment and hurries out of the room.*) The Director . . . son of a bitch. . . .

THE GUARD. (*Yelling after him.*) Main floor to the left of the Check Room.

JEAN-CLAUDE. (*Pointing to his catalogue.*) Regards Françoise, un photo d'artiste . . .

FRANÇOISE. (*Looking at it.*) Tiens. . . .

THE GUARD. (*To himself.*) I still don't understand how he got past the attendant downstairs.

FRANÇOISE. Quelle bouche!

JEAN-CLAUDE. (*Looking closely at the picture.*) C'est une bouche. . . . extraordinaire!

THE GUARD. I mean, Raoul is tough on photographers!

FRANÇOISE. Une peu . . . chimpanzé, n'est-ce-pas?

JEAN-CLAUDE. Chimpanzé?

FRANÇOISE. Mais oui, chimpanzé!

JEAN-CLAUDE. Mais voyons Françoise, qu'est-ce que tu veux dire? Que C'est artiste extraordinaire resemble. . . . un chimpanzé? Un bête sauvage? (*Looks at the picture, more and more troubled.*) C'est une erreur, une faute de photographe . . . (*Looks closer.*) C'est . . . *incroyable!*

FRANÇOISE. Eh? Eh?

JEAN-CLAUDE. (*Approaches* THE GUARD *with his catalogue opened to the page, in pigeon English.*) Excuse me please. The photograph in my catalogue. Here. This picture of Zachery Moe. There must be some mistake. This is a photo of a chimpanzee!

THE GUARD. Chimpanzee? (*Takes the catalogue and looks.*)

JEAN-CLAUDE. You see, that is not a photograph of the artist. It's a photograph of a chimpanzee!

FRANÇOISE. (*Leaning over* THE GUARD's *shoulder.*) C'est toute à fait fantastique!

THE GUARD. (*Looking at the picture very closely.*) It sure looks like a chimpanzee.

FRANÇOISE. (*Delighted, breaks into a light giggle, makes a slight monkey chattering noise.*)

JEAN-CLAUDE. (*Snatching the catalogue away from* THE GUARD.) Monsieur, I am shocked. I have never seen such a thing before. Such an insult as this! You should be ashamed!

FRANÇOISE. C'est absolument ridicule!

JEAN-CLAUDE. It's a disgrace. . . .

FRANÇOISE. (*Chatters in his ear, teasing, laughing.*)

JEAN-CLAUDE. (*Realizes how foolish it all is, succumbs and joins her in an answering chatter. Never for a moment do they abandon their French precision or dignity.*)

ANNETTE FROEBEL. (*Enters. She can be any woman of any age. She looks around, confused.*) Where did the Colonial Quilts and Weathervanes go?

THE GUARD. (*Shaking his head.*) No, that was no chimpanzee. I've seen his picture in the papers, and he doesn't look like no chimp!

ANNETTE FROEBEL. (*Remembering them as clear as day.*) Colonial Quilts and Weathervanes used to be in this room . . . right over there!

THE GUARD. Colonial Quilts and Weathervanes are on the third floor, Miss!

ANNETTE FROEBEL. The *third* floor?

THE GUARD. Third floor.

ANNETTE FROEBEL. Are you sure?

THE GUARD. Colonial Quilts and Weathervanes are on the third floor.

ANNETTE FROEBEL. I could have sworn they were on this floor. (*She exits.*)

LIZ'S VOICE. (*Offstage.*) Did you hear what happened to Botticelli's "Venus" this morning?

CAROL'S VOICE. (*Offstage.*) No, what?

LIZ'S VOICE. Some maniac shot it with a gun.

LIZ, CAROL, and BLAKEY. (*Enter, enthusiastic college girls who are taking an art course together.*)

CAROL. Someone *shot* it? People don't shoot paintings. They slash them!

LIZ. I heard it on the radio this morning. A hooded man pumped 18 bullets into the Venus figure at the Uffizi.

CAROL. I've never heard of anyone . . . shooting a painting.

BLAKEY. You're right! They usually attack them with knives or axes.

CAROL. There's something so . . . alienated . . . about shooting a painting.

BLAKEY. . . . and then there was the guy that wrote slogans all over "Guernica" with a can of spray paint!

LIZ. (*Laughing.*) That's right: spray paint!

BLAKEY. Red spray paint . . . and he misspelled everything, remember?

LIZ. (*Leading them to the Moe's.*) Carol, Blakey, guys, YOU'RE GOING TO LOVE HIM! (*They look at his work with reverence.*)

LIZ. (*Softly.*) You know, his parents are deaf mutes
. . . *both* of them . . . profoundly deaf. . . .

BLAKEY and CAROL. (*Gasp.*)

LIZ. Can you imagine what it must have been like
growing up with parents who couldn't hear you? I
mean, when would you figure out that it was *their*
affliction and not yours? How could a baby realize
there was anything unusual about his parents?
(*Pause.*) Since he never heard them utter a word, he
must have assumed he couldn't speak either. He could
hear his own little baby sounds of course, but he had
no idea what they were. . . .

BLAKEY and CAROL. (*Exhale, impressed with the
dilemma.*)

LIZ. When he cried . . . no one heard him. (*Pause.*)

BLAKEY. Maybe he never did cry!

LIZ. Of course he cried! All babies cry. Even deaf
babies.

CAROL. (*Lost.*) He assumed he couldn't speak
either . . . ?

LIZ. Don't forget, his parents could always *see* him
cry. Sooner or later he must have realized that in
order to get their attention he didn't really *have to
cry*, all he had to do was go through the motions. . . .
(*She opens her mouth and cries without making a
sound.*)

BLAKEY. (*Musing.*) If a deaf, *mute* baby had hear-
ing parents . . . they couldn't hear *him* cry either. . . .
(*Pause.*)

CAROL. (*Still lost.*) . . . go through the motions?

LIZ. (*To* BLAKEY.) The deaf aren't necessarily mute,
you know, some of them can make some sort of resid-
ual sound. . . .

CAROL. (*She's got it.*) WHEN HE CRIED. . . .
NO ONE HEARD HIM!

Liz. . . . but it's not the case with Zachery Moe's parents. They are consigned to absolute and life long silence.

Blakey. (*Her head spinning from it all, turns her back on the Moe's and notices the clothesline.*) OH, MY GOD, WILL YOU LOOK AT THAT?! IT'S INCREDIBLE!

Liz. (*Reaching for* Carol.) When Moe finally realized that his meandering attempts at speech fell on deaf ears. . . .

Blakey. (*Pulling* Carol *with her.*) *THIS IS THE MOST BEAUTIFUL THING I'VE EVER SEEN IN MY LIFE!* (*Touching it gently.*)

The Guard. (*To* Blakey.) Please don't handle the art works.

Blakey. It's . . . fantastic!

The Guard. DON'T HANDLE THE ART WORKS!

Blakey. Oh, I'm sorry. (*To* Carol.) Imagine thinking of making a clothesline . . . with the bodies left inside the clothes. . . .

Carol. (*Torn between her two friends.*) Yeah. . . .

Blakey. It's a reality grounded in illusion . . . !

Carol. (*Feeling trapped, detaches herself from* Blakey.) You know, this is the first time I've ever been in this museum!

Blakey. Oh no! There's even a little kid wearing a tee shirt!

The Guard. DON'T TOUCH!

Blakey. I'm not touching, for Christsakes, I'm just looking!

Carol. (*Walking around the room.*) I've lived in this city my whole life, and this is the first time I've ever been to this museum!

BLAKEY. It's our bodies that give our clothes meaning, just as without our clothes we. . . .

CAROL. (*Looking out the window.*) You know, you can always tell the quality of a museum by the view out the windows.

BLAKEY. (*Kneels by the basket of clothespins.*) Do you see this? He even left out the basket of clothespins?!

THE GUARD. (*Walks over to her.*) Please don't handle the basket of clothespins!

BLAKEY. (*Rises.*) If you're not supposed to handle the basket of clothespins, how come the artist put them there?

CAROL. (*To* BLAKEY.) The Tate Gallery has just about the shittiest view of any museum in the world!

BLAKEY. (*To* THE GUARD.) He put them there so we *would* touch them!

CAROL. The view from the Del Prado isn't so hot either.

LIZ. (*Still enthralled with the Moe's.*) He chose painting as his voice! (*Opens her catalogue, stops at a page.*) Look at his early sketches! The drawings he did of his toys when he was only three! Do you believe this technique? Look at his handling of perspective. . . .

JEAN-CLAUDE and FRANÇOISE. (*Have worked their way to the Agnes Vaag sculptures.*)

FRANÇOISE. Jean-Claude, elle resemble Tougache, tu sais?

JEAN-CLAUDE. Il est beaucoup imité, tu sais, Tougache!

FRANÇOISE. C'est le même esprit que Tougache!

JEAN-CLAUDE. Tougache est trop admiré!

FRANÇOISE. C'est une style un peu comme Kavitsky aussi. . . .

JEAN-CLAUDE. Mon chou, tu sais tres bien que je n'aime pas Tougache de tout!

FRANÇOISE. Kavitsky est sombre. . . .

JEAN-CLAUDE. ECOUTE FRANÇOISE, TOUGACHE EST BÊTE!

FRANÇOISE. Elle choisie les objects simples comme Kimoto. . . .

JEAN-CLAUDE. (*Flings down his catalogue in a rage and starts storming around the room.*) TOUGACHE EST DE LA SALOPERIE! JE DETESTE TOUGACHE! TOUGACHE EST DE LA MERDE (*He starts raving in French.*)

FRANÇOISE. (*Upset and embarrassed.*) Jean-Claude . . . cheri. . . . (*They stand at opposite ends of the room, sulking.*)

BLAKEY. The image of people being . . . laundered . . . washed . . . soaking wet . . . pinned up on the clothesline of life to dry out. . . .

CAROL. (*Standing next to a window.*) If I designed a museum, there would be no art on display . . . just windows. The public would come *inside* the museum in order to look *outside* the windows. The object of study would be nature itself . . . as seen through many different types of windows. There'd be . . . elevated windows, dropped windows, stained glass windows, broken windows, bricked up windows, open windows . . . all looking out at exactly the same view. . . .

LIZ. (*Still enthralled in front of the Moe's.*) I don't know which I like more, his landscapes or seascapes. . . .

CAROL. And then there'd be windows that weren't really windows at all, but *paintings* of windows. . . .

BLAKEY. (*Starts laughing in delight over The Clothesline.*)

MR. HOLLINGSFORD. (*Enters. He could be anybody, to* THE GUARD.) Where would I find the . . . uh . . . the uh . . . (*He looks at* BLAKEY *and gets more confused.*) . . . Colonial Quilts and Weathervanes?

THE GUARD. Third floor.

MR. HOLLINGSFORD. Colonial Quilts and Weathervanes.

THE GUARD. Colonial Quilts and Weathervanes are on the third floor!

MR. HOLLINGSFORD. I was told they were on this floor. (*He consults his catalogue.*)

BLAKEY. (*Can't contain her delight over The Clothesline and sways her head back and forth laughing and moaning gently.*)

THE GUARD. "The Broken Silence" is on this floor.

MR. HOLLINGSFORD. What?

THE GUARD. I SAID, "THE BROKEN SILENCE" IS ON THIS FLOOR!

MR. HOLLINGSFORD. Broken . . . what? (*Looks through his catalogue with rising alarm.*)

THE GUARD. SILENCE!

EVERYONE. (*Is startled and instantly quiet.*)

MR. HOLLINGSFORD. Broken quilts?

THE GUARD. Colonial Quilts and Weathervanes is on the third floor.

MICHAEL WALL. (*Re-enters with all his photographic equipment minus the tripod, drops it to the floor underneath "Landscape I" and waves a paper in his hand.*) I got permission from The Director!

THE GUARD. COLONIAL QUILTS AND WEATHERVANES IS ON THE THIRD FLOOR!

BLAKEY. (*Still on the floor, sways and croons with renewed feeling.*)

MICHAEL WALL. I just got permission from the Director himself. You can see, he signed it!

MR. HOLLINGSFORD. (*Bewildered.*) The broken silence?

MICHAEL WALL. He was very nice about it. He took my tripod, but he invited me back to the next show.

THE GUARD. (*To* MR. HOLLINGSFORD.) This is the last day of the show.

MR. HOLLINGSFORD. Thank you very much, I will. (*He exits.*)

MICHAEL WALL. I know it's the last day of the show, that's why I'm here!

BLAKEY. (*Emits a peal of delighted laughter.*)

LIZ. Just as sound and speech were irrelevant to him, so line and form became irrelevant. (*Pause.*) It makes you wonder where he'll go from here. . . . (*She dreams in front of the Moe's.*)

THE GUARD. (*Takes the permission slip from* MICHAEL WALL.) It's against museum regulations to photograph the art works without permission from the Director.

BLAKEY. (*Advances on the clothesline, wedges inbetween two of the figures as if she's part of the work.*) Do you know what this makes me want to do? It makes me want to grab some of the clothespins and pin myself right up there alongside the others. . . . I want to be laundered . . . hung up to dry . . . all limp and dripping wet with the sun slowly drying me out . . .

THE GUARD. (*Going up to her.*) All right, Miss, that's enough. I'm going to have to ask you to leave. . . .

BLAKEY. They look so at peace, cleansed . . . flapping in the sun. . . .

THE GUARD. (*Guiding her out of the room.*) That's it . . . we've had enough . . . quietly, quietly . . . just move it right along. . . .

BLAKEY's VOICE. (*From Offstage.*) I want to join them! I want to be cleansed! I want to feel the sun on my face. . . .

CAROL. And then at some point, the structure of the museum would . . . just end . . . and everyone would suddenly be . . . outside . . . *in the view* . . . they'd actually *become the view*, the objects on display. You'll stand in line and pay admission . . . to see . . . *yourself!* And then the guards will be hired to watch the people . . . watching each other . . . GOD! I'VE GOT TO WRITE THIS DOWN! (*She exits.*)

LIZ. (*Seated before the Moe's, falls into a revery.*) They must be so proud of him, his parents . . . so very proud. (*A silence descends. It's finally broken by:*)

ELIZABETH SORROW. (*A highly sensitive woman who enters. She has tremendous difficulty orienting herself to the art works. She doesn't know how long it takes to "see" them. She flits from one to the next like a frantic bee, or a yo-yo bobbing on a string that keeps getting shorter and shorter. When she's through looking at something she doesn't trust her impressions, but rushes back to it for another glance, then on to the next one to compare, then back again. In the midst of her confusion. . . .*)

PETER ZIFF. (*Enters. A silent and nervous man who glitters with a strange menace. His moves are stealthy and ambiguous. He should give the impression of having visited this show many times. Like* ELIZABETH SORROW, *he rarely notices other people.*)

(*Time passes in absolute silence as they alternately explore their hidden worlds. This silence is finally*

*broken by the sound of a lively voice intoning
on a recorded tour.)*

MR. and MRS. SALT. *(Enter, attached to the recorded
tour and to each other by the twin wires they have
plugged into their ears. They are not experienced
museum-goers and are terrified by the erudition of
the voice babbling into their ears. Furthermore, they've
never worn an accoustaguide before, and keep getting
hopelessly tangled up in all the wires. The machine
hangs around MR. SALT's neck, and MRS. SALT follows
him timidly. They are eventually overwhelmed by the
difficulty of 1) keeping face, 2) following the instruc-
tions of the guide, and 3) maneuvering with all the
wires that keep getting in their way . . . and they collapse on the nearest bench.)*

THIS IS THE TEXT OF THE RECORDED TOUR. On
behalf of the trustees of the Museum, it gives me great
pleasure to welcome you to our current exhibition,
"The Broken Silence." Before we start on our tour, let
me say a few words about the operation of the casette
you are now wearing around your neck. The small
red button on the left allows you to turn me on or
off at your own discretion. When you hear this beep
sound *(Beep sound.)*, it is the signal that my com-
mentary about a specific work is finished and that you
may turn the button to the "off" position and enjoy
the painting or sculpture at your own leisure. When
you wish to rejoin me, simply turn the button back
to "on" and our tour will continue. If you inadvert-
antly miss any of my remarks and would like to hear
them again, switch the red button to "off" and then
turn the adjacent white button to the "replay" position. My comments will then be repeated until you
are caught up and ready to proceed. At that time,

just return the white button to "play" and be sure to remember to flip the red button back to the "on" position. To raise and lower the volume on the earphone element, just turn the large black dial at the center of the casette clockwise or counter-clockwise. If the quality of your recorded tour is defective in any way, simply exchange it for another casette at the front desk, main floor, to the left of the checkroom.

JEAN-CLAUDE and FRANÇOISE. (*Find themselves in front of the clothesline, and are horrified by it.*)

FRANÇOISE. Mon Dieu, Jean-Claude, regards!

JEAN-CLAUDE. Quelle horreur!

FRANÇOISE. C'est affreux!

JEAN-CLAUDE. Un insult!

FRANÇOISE. Dégoutant. . . .

JEAN-CLAUDE. Déplorable. . . .

FRANÇOISE. Débraillé. . . .

JEAN-CLAUDE. Décadent. . . .

FRANÇOISE. Déclassé. . . . (*They get angrier and angrier.*)

JEAN-CLAUDE. Décomposé. . . .

FRANÇOISE. Défectif. . . .

JEAN-CLAUDE. Défoncé. . . . (*And faster and faster.*)

FRANÇOISE. DÉFORMÉ!

JEAN-CLAUDE. DÉGÉNERÉ!

FRANÇOISE. DÉGRADANT!

JEAN-CLAUDE. DÉMODÉ!

FRANÇOISE. (*Weepy.*) Je veux partir, Jean-Claude.

JEAN-CLAUDE. Moi aussi, Françoise. (*He takes her arm and with the utmost grace and disdain . . . they exit.*)

(*At this point the following people are in the gallery.* THE GUARD *watching over* LIZ. LIZ *watching the*

*Zachery Moe's and thumbing through her cat-
alogue.* ELIZABETH SORROW *resting on one of the
benches. The* SALTS *at the mercy of their recorded
tour,* MICHAEL WALL *taking pictures, and* PETER
ZIFF, *moody and restless.*)

MAGGIE SNOW. (*Enters, a woman in a hurry. To*
THE GUARD.) Excuse me, where is the Puritan Pewter
and Hooked Rugs?

THE GUARD. You mean, Colonial Quilts and Weathervanes.

MAGGIE SNOW. No! Puritan Pewter and Hooked
Rugs!

THE GUARD. We don't have Puritan Pewter or
Hooked Rugs on exhibit here, only Colonial Quilts
and Weathervanes!

MAGGIE SNOW. (*Exits, running.*) Typical! Typical!
(*Almost bumping into:*)

BOB LAMB and WILL WILLARD. (*Who glide into the
room like elegant swans. They are experienced
museum-goers, close friends, and arbiters of good
taste.*)

WILL WILLARD. Bruce said the show was shit!

BOB LAMB. Bruce says everything is shit!

WILL WILLARD. Well, Bruce said *this* show was espe-
cially shit. *Merde de la merde!*

BOB LAMB. (*Looking around the room.*) Preten-
tious. . . . ?

WILL WILLARD. This wasn't my idea . . . !

BOB LAMB. (*Looking at the Moe's.*) Ad Reinhardt
was doing those in black twenty years ago!

WILL WILLARD. I would never in a million years. . . .

BOB LAMB. And Yves Klein did them in blue before
you were even born!

WILL WILLARD. I'm sorry, my taste is more. . . .

BOB LAMB. It's pure Rauschenberg, but without the emotion.

WILL WILLARD. Wait a minute, I love Rauschenberg!

BOB LAMB. Willard, I love him too, but . . . *this.* . . .

WILL WILLARD. Rauschenberg is a giant!

BOB LAMB. Rauschenberg is . . . *the* giant!

FRED IZUMI. (*Enters. Another photographer, a second generation Oriental who's been completely Americanized save for a residue of old world politeness. He starts setting up his equipment in front of one of the Moe's.*)

BOB LAMB. (*Looking at the clothesline.*) I like Segal better.

WILL WILLARD. You do?

BOB LAMB. Don't you?

WILL WILLARD. I thought you've said Segal was shallow.

BOB LAMB. I've never said Segal was . . . shallow. Just a bit . . . muted for my taste.

WILL WILLARD. Well, what about Duane Hanson?

BOB LAMB. Hanson . . . (*Laughing with pleasure.*) is divine!

THE GUARD. (*Noticing* FRED IZUMI.) Hey mister, it's against museum regulations to photograph the art works!

WILL WILLARD. Hanson is . . . insane!

FRED IZUMI. (*To* THE GUARD.) Excuse me, but I notice there is another man here taking photographs.

WILL WILLARD. Of course my all-time favorite is . . .

WILL WILLARD. Claes Oldenberg!   BOB LAMB. Claes Oldenberg! I know!

FRED IZUMI. (*Going over to* THE GUARD.) I'm sorry

for troubling you again, but unless I'm very mistaken, that fellow over there is taking photographs.

THE GUARD. He has permission.

FRED IZUMI. Oh . . . he has permission.

BOB LAMB. (*Reads the title of the clothesline.*) "Wet Dream Left Out to Dry, 197 " (*He starts to laugh.*)

WILL WILLARD. (*Laughs with him.*)

BOB LAMB. (*Reading in an affected voice.*) "On loan from the Los Angeles County Museum of Art!"

FRED IZUMI. (*To* THE GUARD.) Would there be some way I might get permission as well?

LIZ. (*Comes out of her revery over the Moe's. Looks around the room for her friends who have disappeared.*) Carol? Blakey? Guys? Hello? CAROL? GUYS? (*She exits in a panic.*)

WILL WILLARD. Isn't it terribly loud in here? I can't see a thing!

BOB LAMB. This has always been a noisy museum.

FRED IZUMI. If there is some procedure to follow to get permission, perhaps you'd tell me what it is.

THE GUARD. If you want permission to photograph the art works, you'll have to see the Director.

FRED IZUMI. Oh, the Director?! That's curious, usually it's the Administrative Assistant who authorizes permission to photograph the art works. (*He exits.*)

BOB LAMB. Oh no, look at that! He put a basket of real clothespins under an imaginary clothesline! Now, that's what I call . . . *panache!*

WILL WILLARD. You mean, *pastiche!*

BOB LAMB. *Pastiche?*

WILL WILLARD. Real clothespins under an imaginary clothesline!

BOB LAMB. Willard, *pastiche* is collage, I mean, *panache* . . . dash!

WILL WILLARD. Robert, the word is . . . *panacea!*

BOB LAMB. *Panacea . . . ?*

WILL WILLARD. No wait, *paradigm!*

BOB LAMB. (*Thinking back, confused.*) *Pastiche . . . ?*

WILL WILLARD. (*Also confused.*) *Placebo . . . ?*

BOB LAMB. PARADIGM . . . ?

FRED IZUMI. (*Reappears, to* THE GUARD, *slightly out of breath.*) Excuse me again, but . . . uh . . . where would I . . . uh . . . find the Director?

THE GUARD. Main floor, to the left of the Checkroom.

FRED IZUMI. Yes of course! The main floor! (*He exits again.*)

BOB LAMB. (*Absent mindedly picks up one of the clothespins to help him find the mot juste.*)

THE GUARD. Please don't handle the clothespins!

BOB LAMB. (*Drops it.*) Oh, sorry. (*To* WILLARD, *but also taunting* THE GUARD.) Did you read that the Metropolitan Museum of Art is only going to be open four days a week?

WILL WILLARD. The Metropolitan?

BOB LAMB. (*To* THE GUARD, *pointedly.*) The museum doesn't have enough money to pay its force of 227 security guards.

WILL WILLARD. The Metropolitan has 227 security guards?

BOB LAMB. (*Eying* THE GUARD.) The Metropolitan *had* 227 security guards. They just let 82 go.

WILL WILLARD. I had no idea the Metropolitan had 227 security guards.

BOB LAMB. They just let 82 go.

WILL WILLARD. I thought they had 50 or 60 guards . . . but *227?!*

BOB LAMB. All the museums are being forced to cut back.

WILL WILLARD. 227 security guards is alot of people!

BOB LAMB. They don't have enough money to meet operating costs anymore.

WILL WILLARD. Robert, 227 security guards is a crowd!

BOB LAMB. They're all closing down a few days during the week.

WILL WILLARD. Jesus!

BOB LAMB. That's right, "Jesus!" Pretty soon there won't be any fucking culture left!

MIRA ZADAL. (*Enters, she's very pretty and flirtatious. She sidles up to* THE GUARD.) Hello. Where are the Museum Engagement calendars sold?

THE GUARD. (*Sweating under her gaze.*) In the Museum Gift Shop. Main floor, to the left of the Check Room.

MIRA ZADAL. (*Starts to exit.*) Thank you so much.

FIRST MAN IN PASSING. (*Rushing through the room on the way to somewhere else.*) Did you hear what happened to Botticelli's Venus this morning?

SECOND MAN IN PASSING. No.

FIRST MAN IN PASSING. Shot and killed with a gun!

SECOND MAN IN PASSING. Shot and . . . *killed?*

FIRST MAN IN PASSING. Shot right off the face of the painting!

SECOND MAN IN PASSING. (*As they both exit.*) Son of a bitch!

MIRA ZADAL. (*Re-enters, sashays up to* THE GUARD.) Do you also have reproductions of ancient Egyptian jewelry in the Museum Gift Shop?

THE GUARD. (*Blushing.*) Books, catalogues, foreign publications, post cards, blown . . . glass. . . .

MIRA ZADAL. (*With a tremulous sigh.*) . . . blown . . . glass?

THE GUARD. (*With rising ardor.*) Pewter figurenes, ceramic reproductions, needlepoint kits, table linens . . . dried flowers. . . .

MIRA ZADAL. (*Groans.*)

THE GUARD. Silver ladels, cloisonné key rings, solid gold cuff links . . . rare spices!

MIRA ZADAL. Oooooooh, you're so . . . helpful! (*She exits.*)

THE GUARD. Main floor, just a little bit left of the Check Room!

ELIZABETH SORROW. (*Exits in her fashion, trying to make doubly sure she has taken everything in.*)

PETER ZIFF. (*Then starts stalking the same art works ELIZABETH has just left. He's bothered by them, but for more destructive and obscure reasons.*)

THE GUARD. (*Watches him like a hawk.*)

PETER ZIFF. (*Frustrated by this scrutiny, sits down on one of the benches.*)

(*A silence into which step:*)

BARBARA ZIMMER and BARBARA CASTLE. (*Enormously stylish mirror images of each other. They have come to the show to be seen and display themselves with langorous grace.*)

BARBARA CASTLE. Gloria said the show was wonderful!

BARBARA ZIMMER. Gloria would!

BARBARA CASTLE. She came to the opening with Misha.

BARBARA ZIMMER. I saw Misha last week!

BARBARA CASTLE. Really?

BARBARA ZIMMER. He was wearing his fur cape!

BARBARA CASTLE. Oh, I love that cape! Did he have on his linen vest with it?

BARBARA ZIMMER. The linen vest . . . *and* an incredible raw silk shirt!

BARBARA CASTLE. Oooooooooh, what color? *What color?*

BARBARA ZIMMER. Bright . . . green!

BARBARA CASTLE. Perfect!

BARBARA ZIMMER. . . . and his tweed cap . . .

BARBARA CASTLE. He was wearing his tweed cap?

BARBARA ZIMMER. Yes!

BARBARA CASTLE. But not his tan boots . . .

BARBARA ZIMMER. . . . not his tan boots. . . .
(*Pause.*)

BARBARA ZIMMER. His   BARBARA CASTLE. His
black ones! (*A groan.*)   black ones! (*A groan.*)
(*Pause.*)

BARBARA CASTLE. What I wouldn't give for that linen vest of his!

BARBARA ZIMMER. Well, you'd have to give a great deal, believe me!

BARBARA CASTLE. Can you see that vest with my gaberdine slacks?!

BARBARA ZIMMER. Barbara, they don't *make* linen like that anymore!

BARBARA CASTLE. Or, with my Halston skirt. . . .

BARBARA ZIMMER. There's a world-wide shortage of natural fibers. We have quite simply used them all up.

BARBARA CASTLE. And it's reversable too. On the inside, it's a lightweight cream wool!

BARBARA ZIMMER. Drained them. . . . .

BARBARA CASTLE. Reversed, I could wear it with practically anything!

BARBARA ZIMMER. Barbara, within the next few years, all our fabric will be synthetic.

BARBARA CASTLE. *Synthetic?* Did you just say, "*synthetic*," Barbara?

BARBARA ZIMMER. Yes, Barbara, I just said, *"synthetic,"* Barbara! They hardly grow any cotton in the South anymore, it's just too expensive to harvest.

BARBARA CASTLE. Barbara, I can't wear synthetics!

BARBARA ZIMMER. Who can, Barbara? WHO CAN?!

BARBARA CASTLE. Last week I bought a slip I was told was pure silk, only to read the label two days later and discover it was Cresulon. Do you know what Cresulon does to my skin?

BARBARA ZIMMER. Chinese silk worms are as scarce as hen's teeth!

BARBARA CASTLE. It coats it with a thin layer of petroleum!

BARBARA ZIMMER. . . . and as for wool. Because the cost of feeding sheep has skyrocketed, the sheep farmers are going bankrupt. Soon, there will be no more wool, cashmere, or angora!

BARBARA CASTLE. Barbara, I've got a rash. A white rash all over my body!

BARBARA ZIMMER. From now on, it's the man-made substitutes: Orlon Acrylic, Lycra Spandex, Quiana Nylon, Fortrel Polyester, and Celanese Arnel Triacetate!

BARBARA CASTLE. And it won't go away! I've tried everything. Barbara, I'm desperate!

(*Pause.*)

BOB LAMB. As the costs of running museums keeps rising, the price of admission is bound to go up. Museums officials are now talking about $10 as a fixed single admission fee.

WILL WILLARD. *$10 to get into the Metropolitan?*

BOB LAMB. $10 for admission into the Metropolitan will be a bargain, Willard, it will be 25 before the end of the decade. The only way people will be able to

afford visiting museums in the future will be in chartered groups!

WILL WILLARD. Chartered groups??! Robert, I go
to the Met by myself, or I don't go at all!

BOB LAMB. The $50 "Budget" Chartered Tour will
include admission into the Metropolitan, the Modern,
and the Whitney. . . .

WILL WILLARD. I would *pay* $50 to avoid a "Bud-
get" Chartered Tour. . . .

BOB LAMB. The "Imperial" Chartered Tour will
include those three, and for $25 more, admission into
the Guggenheim, Cooper-Hewitt, and the Hayden
Planetarium!

WILL WILLARD. Stop, stop!

BOB LAMB. And don't think the private galleries
aren't hurting either. . . .

WILL WILLARD. I have to be alone with the things
I love!

BOB LAMB. The day will come when you'll have to
use Master Charge to get into Pace and Castelli!

WILL WILLARD. The Morgan Collection of Renaissance jewels, snuff boxes, and enameled jeweled
cups. . . . !

BOB LAMB. Write checks for admittance into second
story Soho galleries!

WILL WILLARD. Do you *know* the Morgan Collection at the Met? Have you ever *seen* the Rospigliosi
Cup?

BOB LAMB. Pay cash to . . .

WILL WILLARD. Robert, when I stand before that
cup, I can't stand two people within 10 feet of me!
(*Pause.*)

BARBARA CASTLE. (*To* BARBARA ZIMMER.) This is
the first time I've ever had a . . . *white* rash!

WILL WILLARD. (*To* BOB LAMB.) The last time I

was there, there was a swarm . . . of screaming children.

BARBARA CASTLE. (*Revealing some bare arm.*) Look! (*She blows on it, a fine white powder rises.*) Did you see that?

WILL WILLARD. I broke out in a sweat. . . .

BARBARA CASTLE. I think I'm on fire. . . .

WILL WILLARD. It's called Agoraphobia!

BARBARA CASTLE. It keeps getting worse!

WILL WILLARD. I'm told it's incurable. . . .

BARBARA CASTLE. . . . and Barbara, it's spreading!

(*A pause.*)

BARBARA ZIMMER. (*To* BARBARA CASTLE.) The handwriting is on the wall!

BOB LAMB. (*To* WILL WILLARD.) Our troubles have just begun!

BARBARA ZIMMER. (*Agreeing with* BOB LAMB, *but for her own reasons.*) We could lose everything!

BOB LAMB. (*To* BARBARA ZIMMER.) Exactly!

BARBARA ZIMMER. (*To* BOB LAMB.) We're only beginning to wake up . . .

BOB LAMB. . . . and when we finally do, it will be too late!

BARBARA ZIMMER. Of course, this is not the first time.

BOB LAMB. No, we've been through it before.

BARBARA CASTLE. This is the first time I've ever had a white rash!

WILL WILLARD. I just hope we can retain what's most precious to us.

BARBARA ZIMMER. We've tried so hard!

BOB LAMB. Sacrificed so much. . . .

BARBARA CASTLE. Given our all. . . .

WILL WILLARD. Gone more than halfway. . . .

BARBARA ZIMMER. Stinted on nothing. . . .

BOB LAMB. Held out for the best.

BARBARA CASTLE. Fought a fair fight. . . .

WILL WILLARD. And stuck to our guns!

(*A pause.*)

BARBARA ZIMMER. He's right!

BOB LAMB. You said it!

BARBARA CASTLE. Well put!

WILL WILLARD. Culture, as we know it. . . .

BOB LAMB. Is on the way out!

BARBARA ZIMMER. On the way out. . . .

BARBARA CASTLE. . . . and disappearing round the bend!

(*A pause.*)

THE GUARD. (*Suddenly launches into a tap dance of private protest. It rises in spirit and magnificence. Everyone watches him in amazement. The* SALTS *start to applaud and then check the gauche impulse. The dance suddenly stops and* THE GUARD *returns to his post as if nothing happened. To himself.*) It's the last day of the show. (*Everyone resumes their former activities and the room falls into silence.*)

MR. GREGORY. (*Enters, a shy man with a recorded tour that's playing much too loud.*)

THE RECORDED TOUR. ON BEHALF OF THE TRUSTEES AND ADMINISTRATION OF THE MUSEUM, IT GIVES ME GREAT PLEASURE TO WELCOME YOU TO OUR CURRENT EXHIBITION, 'THE BROKEN SILENCE.' FIRST, LET ME SAY A FEW WORDS ABOUT THE OPERATION OF. . . .

EVERYONE. (*Eyes him with hostility, their hands over their ears.*)

THE GUARD. WILL YOU PLEASE TURN THAT DOWN?

WILL WILLARD. WHAT'S GOING ON IN HERE?

BOB LAMB. I TOLD YOU THIS WAS A NOISY MUSEUM!

MICHAEL WALL. HEY MISTER. . . .

THE BARBARAS. (*Shake their heads and cluck.*)

FRED IZUMI. (*Re-enters, goes up to* THE GUARD, *hands him a slip.*) My permission slip from The Director! (*He sets his gear down by the Moe's.*)

THE GUARD. *WHAT?*

FRED IZUMI. PERMISSION SLIP FROM THE DIRECTOR!

THE GUARD. I SAID, IT'S AGAINST MUSEUM REGULATIONS TO PHOTOGRAPH THE ART WORKS!

FRED IZUMI. MAIN FLOOR TO THE LEFT OF THE CHECK ROOM!

THE GUARD. THE GUARD DOWNSTAIRS. . . .

FRED IZUMI. YES, I SAW THE DIRECTOR. . . .

THE RECORDED TOUR. (*Mysteriously regulates itself on, "Yes, I saw the Director,"*)

THE GUARD. IT'S AGAINST. . . .

MR. GREGORY. (*Somehow manages to turn the sound completely off.*)

FRED IZUMI. (*Hands* THE GUARD *his slip.*) My permission slip from the Director.

THE GUARD. (*Taking it.*) Wonderful!

FRED IZUMI. Main floor, to the left of the check room!

THE GUARD. . . . terrific!

MR. and MRS. SALT. (*Their recorded tour suddenly goes beserk in sympathy with* MR. GREGORY'S. *It plays insanely loud and then very very fast.*)

EVERYONE. (*Groans and mutters in angry disbelief.*)

THE GUARD. LOOK. . . . WOULD YOU PLEASE TURN DOWN THE VOLUME. . . .

MR. GREGORY. (*Cowering in a corner.*) THE SAME

THING HAPPENED TO MINE, JUST SHAKE IT . . . (*Etc.*)

MR. and MRS. SALT. (*Terrified and frantic with embarrassment bang on the controls.*)

| MRS. SALT. TURN THE RED BUTTON, NOT THE WHITE BUTTON. . . . NO, NO . . . *THIS* ONE. . . . NOT SO FAR. . . . | MR. SALT. SOMETHING'S GONE WRONG SOMEWHERE!! I'M TURNING THE WHITE BUTTON, BUT NOTHING HAPPENS. . . . GOD DAMNED MACHINE. . . ! |

THE GUARD. LOOK, I'M GOING TO HAVE TO ASK YOU TO LEAVE! (*Strong arms* MR. SALT *out of the room.*)

MRS. SALT. (*Is pulled helplessly after him on her attached wire.*)

PETER ZIFF. (*Seizes the moment and quickly rushes over to one of the Moe's, takes out a small pencil and scribbles intensely on one small corner. With sweat pouring down his face, he looks to see if anyone saw him, and then quietly sneaks out of the room.*)

FRED IZUMI. (*To* THE GUARD.) Both he and his assistant were very courteous. It turns out we have mutual friends in Cincinnati. (*He then paces down the length of all the Moe's, reading their titles out loud to himself.*) "Landscape I, 197 . Acrylic emulsion and wax on canvas. On loan from the Sidney Rubin Gallery."

BOB LAMB. (*To* WILL WILLARD.) Not only will it cost $10 to get into the Metropolitan, but because of the shortage of guards, certain galleries will be roped off on odd and even days of the month.

FRED IZUMI. "Landscape II, 197 . Acrylic emulsion and wax on canvas. On loan from the Sidney Rubin Gallery."

BOB LAMB. Medieval helmets will only be on view even days, from noon til one. Renaissance stringed instruments, odd days, from two to three.

FRED IZUMI. "Seascape VII, 197 . Acrylic emulsion and wax on canvas. On loan from the Sidney Rubin Gallery."

BOB LAMB. Sooner or later, the less popular exhibits will close altogether: Etruscan bronzes, Mid-Eastern glazed bricks. . . .

FRED IZUMI. "Starscape 19, 197 . Acrylic emulsion and wax on canvas, on loan from the artist."

BOB LAMB. Eventually, entire periods and forms of art will be lost completely as the public is denied access!

FRED IZUMI. (*Amazed.*) "On loan from the . . . *artist?!*"

BOB LAMB. One by one, all the treasures of Western civilization will be dismanteled, put into storage . . . lowered into fibre glass crates and buried under ground . . . to be grouped and catalogued by art historians wearing thick, lint-free, asbestos gloves. (*Pause.*) We will never again stand face to face with an original painting or sculpture. And if there is no place where that painting or sculpture can be shown, the artist is bound to ask: *Who am I doing it for . . . And why am I doing it?* The impulse to create will be shattered. Willard, this may be our last day in the presence of live art!

WILL WILLARD. Wait a minute! Yesterday I was standing one foot away from probably *the* most live and stunning object of art made by man in the last 400 years! Robert, have you ever studied the Rospig-

liosi Cup? It's a fucking dazzler! (*Pause.*) It's this
. . . incredible scalloped sea shell which rests on the
back of an enameled dragon . . . which in turn rests
on the back of an enameled turtle. It's carved out of
solid gold and is no more than 10 inches high and 8
inches across. Instead of a handle, a winged sphinx
perches on the rim of the cup, a gigantic baroque pearl
hanging between her golden breasts. I mean, the work-
manship, the detail . . . the fantasy! Tiny seed pearl
earrings dangle from her ears . . . and instead of having the traditional legs and paws of a lion . . . she
has flippers! Indigo blue flippers etched in enamel.
You can *count* each irredescent scale!

BOB LAMB. Well, you'd better get ready to kiss it
goodbye . . . it won't be there in two weeks. All the
museums are closing.

WILL WILLARD. Robert, what on earth are you talking about?

BOB LAMB. The museums . . . are . . . shutting
. . . down!

WILL WILLARD. Robert, no museums are shutting
down.

BOB LAMB. Willard, we've got to do something!

(*As* BOB LAMB *is tensed for some sort of desperate act,
there's a gradual slowing down of movement and
speech. As a group, the visitors in the museum
become languid art works themselves.* THE GUARD
paces, MICHAEL WALL *keeps taking pictures,* FRED
IZUMI *prepares to take his,* MR. GREGORY *dog-
gedly follows his tour, the* BARBARAS *pluck at
each other's beautiful clothes, and* WILL WILLARD
*stares straight ahead. This moment of serenity is
broken as:*)

CHLOE TRAPP. (*Enters. She's on the curatorial staff of the museum. Her life and passion center on discovering and explaining the mysteries of modern art.*)

ADA BILDITSKY. (*Enters with her, a patron of the arts who's being given a special private tour.*)

LIZ. (*Suddenly careens into the room, unconscious of everyone.*) Carol? Blakey? Guys? (*She exits.*)

CHLOE TRAPP. This is the final day of our group show, "The Broken Silence," and here we have the work of an extraordinary young Post-Conceptual painter, Zachery Moe.

EVERYONE. (*Looks up at the sound of her voice. They are held by her seriousness and authority.*)

CHLOE TRAPP. Most significant painting since Matisse's "Joie de Vivre," has been reductive. Reductivism does not belong to any one style: it is as operative in painting conceived as a gesture . . . as in painting cut down to a line or square. The traditional aim of reduction has been to push painting to its farthest limits by reducing it to its bare essentials. In slicing away residues of imagry that have lost their relevance, the artist seeks to transform the apple . . . into a diamond.

(*A pause.*)

ADA BILDITSKY. I'm so grateful!

EVERYONE EXCEPT THE GUARD. (*Instinctively gathers around* CHLOE TRAPP *for more.*)

BARBARA CASTLE. Oh, we're all so grateful!

WILL WILLARD. *I'm* grateful!

BOB LAMB. No one . . . is more grateful than me!

MR. GREGORY. I had no idea anyone was going to. . . .

FRED IZUMI. Thank you very much.

CHLOE TRAPP. (*Moves to the next Moe.*) There is left the void—not Yves Klein's empty sky, but a void that seeks the cancellation of art as it has been until now and supplanting it with works from which adulterating impulses have been . . . purged. It is evident that Moe saw that a traditional commitment to the theoretical picture plane was no longer relevant.

ADA BILDITSKY. Absolutely evident and no longer relevant.

EVERYONE. (*Except* THE GUARD *who's lost in the rhythms of his own job.*) Absolutely evident and no longer relevant.

CHLOE TRAPP. For such American artists, the concern was mainly with the surface of the canvas and the nature of the pigment applied to it. What states more plainly the literal character of the picture support covered by canvas . . . than a piece of canvas . . . covering that picture support . . . *painted white?!* If the first mark on a surface destroys its flatness, then Moe contradicts this by painting a picture whose first and *only* mark . . . is an all-over white one.

ADA BILDITSKY. (*Letting it sink in.*) All-over white!

EVERYONE. (*Understanding, joyous.*) All-over white!

CHLOE TRAPP. White . . . of course, is the one color carrying in it the potential for all other colors.

(*A pause. These colors should then spill out rapid fire creating a luscious rainbow.*)

ADA BILDITSKY. Red!
MICHAEL WALL. Yellow!
FRED IZUMI. Orange!
BARBARA CASTLE. Violet!
BARBARA ZIMMER. Blue!
BOB LAMB. Green!
WILL WILLARD. Sepia!

MR. GREGORY. Purple!

ADA BILDITSKY. (*Breathing deeply, their favorite colors.*) Rose!

MICHAEL WALL. Turquoise!

FRED IZUMI. Umber!

BARBARA CASTLE. Mauve!

BARBARA ZIMMER. Lavender!

BOB LAMB. Cobalt!

WILL WILLARD. Magenta!

MR. GREGORY. Saffron!

CHLOE TRAPP. The difference between historic Dada and the current fundamentalist version lies in the treatment of the spectator. . . . (*With the word "spectator," everyone turns and faces* CHLOE, *suddenly self conscious that they are the spectators she's talking about.*) Instead of goading you into indignation at the desecreation of art, the new Dada converts you into an aesthete.

EVERYONE. (*Flattered, congratulates themselves, murmuring,* "aesthete.")

CHLOE TRAPP. The monotonous shapes and bleak surfaces presented to you as objects wrapped in their own being compel you to embrace a professional sensitivity to contrasts of tone, light, and dimension. The more a work is purged of inessentials, the closer the scrutiny required to see it . . . and the more precious the sensibility required to respond to it!

(*A reverential silence.*)

ADA BILDITSKY. Oh, you were just . . . wonderful! Really . . . wonderful!

EVERYONE. (*Breaks into applause.*)

CHLOE TRAPP. (*Suddenly made shy by their outpouring, ducks her head to one side, and rushes from the room.*) How kind . . . you're too kind. . . .

ADA BILDITSKY. I've never heard anything so . . .

lyrical . . . so inspired . . . so informative . . . so apt! (*She runs after* CHLOE.)

EVERYONE. (*Is stirred by their new vision. They move around the Moe's, not daring to speak for fear of breaking the spell.*)

GILDA NORRIS. (*Enters, intense and serious, she carries a folding chair and sketch book. She settles down in front of one of the Moe's and starts copying it with as much fury as if she were reproducing a Rembrandt.*)

THE GUARD. I'm sorry miss, it's against museum regulations to sketch from the art works!

GILDA NORRIS. I can't sketch without permission from the Director?

THE GUARD. I didn't tell you it was the Director who gave permission to sketch. How did you know the Director gives permission to sketch?

GILDA NORRIS. Because I have sketching permission from the Director.

THE GUARD. You have *sketching* permission from the Director? I've never seen sketching permission from the Director!

GILDA NORRIS. I'm the Director's daughter!

THE GUARD. Oh, you're the Director's *daughter*. . . .

GILDA NORRIS. . . . the sketching Director's daughter. . . .

THE GUARD. (*Laughs.*) . . . sketching Director's daughter. . . .

GILDA NORRIS. (*Still sketching.*) The . . . *fetching*, sketching Director's daughter!

THE GUARD. (*Laughs light heartedly.*)

GILDA NORRIS. The . . . *letching*, fetching, sketching Director's daughter!

THE GUARD. (*Laughs, with embarrassment.*)

BOB LAMB. Willard, now's the time to make our

move. See that basket of clothespins over there, I'm going to steal one dozen of them!

GILDA NORRIS. (*Rises and advances on* THE GUARD.) The . . . *kvetching*, letching, fetching, sketching Director's daughter!

WILL WILLARD. Robert, you're crazy!

BOB LAMB. (*Checking that* THE GUARD *is engrossed with* GILDA NORRIS, *starts stuffing clothespins in his pocket.*)

WILL WILLARD. Robert, please!

THE GUARD. (*Rushes over to them.*) HEY, WHAT'S GOING ON OVER HERE? I TOLD YOU, YOU ARE NOT TO TOUCH THE CLOTHESPINS! THEY ARE PART OF THE SCULPTURE!

BOB LAMB. For your information, this is not a "sculpture," it's a "construction."

WILL WILLARD. I'm so embarrassed!

THE GUARD. I DON'T CARE WHAT YOU CALL IT, MISTER, IT'S AGAINST MUSEUM REGULATIONS TO TOUCH THE ART WORKS. NOW, PUT THOSE CLOTHESPINS BACK!

BOB LAMB. Are you accusing me of . . . theft?

THE GUARD. All I said was, put the clothespins back!

BOB LAMB. (*Tossing them back into the basket.*) I hope you realize this is the first time a museum guard has *ever* raised his voice to me. . . .

WILL WILLARD. The poor man is just doing his job!

BOB LAMB. And let me assure you, I've been to every major art museum across the country! The Hirschorn, the Carnegie Institute, the Philadelphia Museum of Art, the Walker Art Center. . . .

THE GUARD. ALL BACK. PUT THEM ALL BACK!

BOB LAMB. Furthermore, this is just about the worst show I've ever seen, anywhere! Real stinko!

WILL WILLARD. Rooooooooooooobert. . . .

BOB LAMB. I'd be embarrassed to work here!

THE GUARD. COME ON, HURRY IT UP! (*Clamping his hands on* BOB LAMB.) Each one of those pins is a valuable piece of art!

BOB LAMB. *You touched me!* That does it! (*He throws back the last remaining ones.*) I'm reporting you to the Director of the Museum. . . .

BOB LAMB. . . . main	THE GUARD. . . . main
floor, to the left of the	floor, to the left of the
Checkroom!	Checkroom!

BOB LAMB. (*Exiting.*) Bruce said this show was shit!

WILL WILLARD. (*Following him.*) BRUCE IS AN ASS HOLE!

THE GUARD. This is just the beginning, just the beginning. . . .

BARBARA ZIMMER. (*Gazing at "Landscape I."*) Barbara, I want one!

BARBARA CASTLE. They are lovely!

BARBARA ZIMMER. *This* one!

BARBARA CASTLE. (*Considering it.*) Mmmmmmmm-mm. . . .

BARBARA ZIMMER. It would be perfect in my bedroom!

BARBARA CASTLE. (*Indicating "Seascape VII."*) *That's* the one for your bedroom, Barbara. This one's more more for your family room.

BARBARA ZIMMER. Are you crazy, Barbara? It would be terrible in the family room!

BARBARA CASTLE. Well, it would be heaven in *my* family room!

BARBARA ZIMMER. Your family room and my family room are two very different places!

BARBARA CASTLE. (*Pointing to "Landscape II."*) *That's* the one for your bedroom, Barbara!

BARBARA ZIMMER. You mean, that's the one for *your* bedroom. . . .

BARBARA CASTLE. (*Gazing at "Landscape II," picturing it in her bedroom.*) No. (*Then looking at the others, settling on "Starscape 19."*) That's the one for my bedroom, and . . . (*After considering, indicating "Landscape I."*) . . . *this* is the one for your family room!

BARBARA ZIMMER. Well, what about *my* bedroom?

BARBARA CASTLE. Barbara, these aren't easy decisions!

BARBARA ZIMMER. (*Pulling her arm.*) Come on, we've got to get out of here. The cafeteria's probably jammed. We'll be in line forever!

BARBARA CASTLE. (*Exiting with her.*) What are you going to order?

BARBARA ZIMMER. Oh, I don't know, I feel like a quiche. . . .

BARBARA CASTLE. I'm more in the mood for a salad.

BARBARA ZIMMER. Their spinach salads are excellent!

BARBARA CASTLE. (*As they exit.*) Yes, I know. . . .

BARBARA CASTLE. Tarragon and dill dressing . . .	BARBARA ZIMMER. Tarragon and dill dressing . . .

MR. GREGORY'S TOUR. (*Suddenly goes beserk again, louder and faster than before. He pounds on it.*)

EVERYONE. (*Looks at him and groans.*)

THE GUARD. HEY, WILL YOU TURN THAT DOWN? LISTEN, I'M AFRAID YOU'RE GOING TO HAVE TO TAKE	MR. GREGORY. IT'S STUCK, THE BUTTON'S STUCK. . . . IT'S JAMMED. . . . I CAN'T. . . . WHAT? I CAN'T

THAT BACK DOWN   TURN IT OFF. . . .
TO THE DESK AND   YES, I'M TRYING,
GET ANOTHER ONE   I'M TRYING, BUT
. . . MAIN FLOOR.   IT'S JAMMED. . . .
. . . I SAID, *MAIN*
FLOOR . . . TO THE
LEFT OF THE . . .

THE GUARD. (*Drags* MR. GREGORY *from the room.*)

TINK SOLHEIM and KATE SIV. (*Enter. They're friends of the artist, Agnes Vaag. They're dressed in exotic yet flattering clothes, and both exude a high strung sensitivity. They've come to the show practically every day.*)

TINK SOLHEIM. . . . the last day of the show!

KATE SIV. I can't believe it! The last day!

THE GUARD. (*Has returned, worn out from* MR. GREGORY.) Last day.

TINK SOLHEIM. The last day!

KATE SIV. Ed called this morning, he said Aggie might come.

TINK SOLHEIM. I know . . .

KATE SIV. He thinks she'll come around noon and bring Hilton with her.

TINK SOLHEIM. That's odd, Hilton told me it would be closer to three.

KATE SIV. No, Ed said Aggie has some appointment later on.

TINK SOLHEIM. Hilton didn't mention anything about it to me.

KATE SIV. Hilton probably hasn't been in touch with Ed.

TINK SOLHEIM. Aggie's busy at noon.

KATE SIV. Not according to Ed.

TINK SOLHEIM. But Aggie would never call Ed!

KATE SIV. You mean, Hilton would never call Ed!

TINK SOLHEIM. Well of course *Hilton* would never call Ed. . . .

KATE SIV. Neither would Aggie.

TINK SOLHEIM. That's true.

KATE SIV. (*Getting depressed.*) She'd never call Hilton, either.

TINK SOLHEIM. But Hilton called *her!*

KATE SIV. She'd never call anyone!

TINK SOLHEIM. . . . and then he called *me!*

KATE SIV. She's the problem!

TINK SOLHEIM. Ed's the problem.

KATE SIV. . . . and I don't trust Hilton.

TINK SOLHEIM. She'll come.

KATE SIV. What time is it?

TINK SOLHEIM. She'll be here.

KATE SIV. Maybe she already came and left. . . .

TINK SOLHEIM. (*In front of one of her pieces.*) Every time I see her work, it moves me more than the last time.

CHLOE TRAPP. (*Enters again with:*)

BILL PLAID. (*A man who is bewildered by art, and enfuriated by modern art. That he is* CHLOE's *guest is the result of some horrible mixup.*)

CHLOE TRAPP. (*Advances to the clothesline.*) This is the final day of our group show, "The Broken Silence." (*Pause.*) In his earliest work, Steve Williams experimented with such typically surrealist devices as totemic imagry, often incorporating assemblages of unrelated objects. The idea of indicating a magically demarcated environment . . . (*She indicates the length of the clothesline.*) for his sculptures, appeared early in his work as did his reliance on cloth and rope for basic materials.

BILL PLAID. (*Confused and depressed.*) Yes. Cloth and rope.

CHLOE TRAPP. A surrealist cast persists in his most recent work, particularly in his use of erotic imagry and in his unexpected variations of color and scale.

TINK SOLHEIM. (*Without knowing what she's doing, picks up one of Agnes Vaag's sculptures and starts caresssing her face with it.*)

BILL PLAID. Yes, highly erotic.

CHLOE TRAPP. What makes Williams' work of unusual contemporary relevance, however, is his attitude towards the materials he uses and the processes he employs.

BILL PLAID. (*Dimly.*) Cloth and rope.

CHLOE TRAPP. Rather than imposing his will upon materials in order to force them into a pre-ordained form, Williams obeys the inherent capabilities of a given material and follows the suggestions offered by its particular qualities.

BILL PLAID. (*Depressed, sits on one of the benches, head in hands.*)

TINK SOLHEIM. (*Is now rubbing the Vaag statue over her face.*)

CHLOE TRAPP. Gesture is a crucial factor in William's work, a means of indicating the participation of the artist in the . . .

KATE SIV. (*Notices that TINK has seized the statue and screams.*)

CHLOE TRAPP. (*Screams because KATE screamed.*)

TINK SOLHEIM. (*Screams because their screams have startled her.*)

BILL PLAID. (*Screams because he can't take it any more.*)

THE GUARD. WHAT'S GOING ON?

KATE SIV. TINK, WHAT ARE YOU DOING WITH AGGIE'S STATUE?

TINK SOLHEIM. (*Lost in her own revery.*) What?

KATE SIV. WHAT . . . ARE . . . YOU . . . DOING? . . .

CHLOE TRAPP. "The Temptation and Curruption of William Blake!"

KATE SIV. It's "The Temptation and Corruption of William Blake!"

TINK SOLHEIM. (*Clutching it tighter.*) No!

CHLOE TRAPP. On loan from the Whitney Museum of American Art.

THE GUARD. Put that statue down, Miss.

CHLOE TRAPP. Her first attempt to combine porous with non-porous objects.

BILL PLAID. (*Groans.*)

KATE SIV. Tink, put it down!

THE GUARD. Please, Miss. . . .

TINK SOLHEIM. (*Feeling cornered, dashes to the clothesline and stands among the bodies.*)

CHLOE TRAPP.	KATE SIV. Oh	FRED IZUMI.
Tink, we'd all	Tink, you're	It's all right,
like you to put	going to drop	Everything's
the statue down	it, and it will	going to be all
before some-	shatter into a	right. . . .
thing terrible	million	
happens . . .	pieces. . . .	

GILDA NORRIS. (*Ready to pounce.*) SURROUND HER!

THE GUARD. Sssssssssh, calm down. Let's everybody just . . . calm down . . . take it easy. . . .

MICHAEL WALL. Hey, could I look at it for a minute? (*Holds out his hands to her with great gentleness.*)

TINK SOLHEIM. (*Eyes him, filled with terror. Starts to soften, reaches out to him.*)

KATE SIV. Oh, Tink, what's happened to you?

THE GUARD. Sssshhhhhh . . .

MICHAEL WALL. I'll give it right back. It's so beautiful. . . .

GILDA NORRIS. GRAB IT!

TINK SOLHEIM. DON'T TOUCH ME!

KATE SIV. Oh Tink. . . .

THE GUARD. Miss, you'd better. . . .

CHLOE TRAPP. It's my favorite one, my very. . . .

BILL PLAID. Go ahead . . . SMASH THE UGLY THING! (*A silence.*)

TINK SOLHEIM. Yesterday . . . I was remembering a day I spent with Agnes Vaag.

KATE SIV. Aggie!

TINK SOLHEIM. . . . Aggie . . .

KATE SIV. We're friends of the artist. *Old* friends . . . she's such a wonderful. . . .

TINK SOLHEIM. Agnes Vaag invited me to spend a day with her in the country. Looking for her things; bones, wings . . . teeth . . .

THE GUARD. (*Reaching up for the statue.*) WATCH IT!

CHLOE TRAPP. ALL OF HER MATERIALS ARE FOUND MATERIALS!

MICHAEL WALL. I've never seen anything like this. . . .

KATE SIV. She'll be here later, with Hilton.

TINK SOLHEIM. She finds all her objects in Connecticut state parks.

TINK SOLHEIM. (*Fitfully caressing her face with the statue.*) At least once a month she gets on a Greyhound bus carrying two blue suitcases filled with soft polyester batting for wrapping her objects in . . . and scours one of Connecticut's state parks. The last time she invited me to go with her. I said I'd bring along an extra suitcase and a picnic lunch. We met at the Port Authority Bus Terminal. It was so . . . odd.

Going with Aggie to look for something. I mean, whenever you see her in her studio, her hands are always full: moulding something, gluing something. Her studio is bursting with the exotic: bird beaks, fish skeletons, turkey down, fox claws. . . .

KATE SIV. I'm Aggie's oldest friend, I've known her for years!

TINK SOLHEIM. So I just assumed she always *had* these things, that they were part of her, not something separate she had to seek out. So it was odd meeting her at Port Authority carrying those two blue suitcases stuffed with polyester batting. . . .

KATE SIV. She's invited me on her expeditions millions of times . . . of course I . . .

TINK SOLHEIM. I don't remember the name of the park we visited, but Aggie seemed to know her way around and before I realized it, we were walking through deep woods. Deep woods is the best place to find small animal skeletons, she told me. While I looked up at the trees and sky, she bent close to the ground, scooping her hands through the underbrush like some human net. In the first hour she found a bat skeleton, several raccoon skulls, a fresh rabbit carcass, patches of fur. . . .

KATE SIV. Aggie's only 24, you know . . . and so beautiful! . . .

TINK SOLHEIM. At one moment she was crouched out of view, the next she was holding fragile white bones up to the sun exclaiming over their perfect . . .

KATE SIV. She has this amazing blonde hair. It's as thick as rope and falls down her back in golden cascades. . . .

TINK SOLHEIM. After awhile she had filled both her blue suitcases and asked if she could borrow mine. We stopped for lunch and she gave me a long speech about how calcium is formed in the bones of vegetarian animals. . . .

KATE SIV. And her eyes are this deep . . . green . . .

TINK SOLHEIM. It wasn't long before my suitcase was filled too and it was starting to get dark. I suggested we walk back along a different route, but she said no, she couldn't stop yet.

KATE SIV. MEN DIE OVER HER!

TINK SOLHEIM. It was then I noticed something . . strange. Well, I didn't notice it, I heard it because it was getting too dark to see. As she was combing the underbrush, I heard this soft kind of . . . licking noise . . . a slight kind of . . . slurping . . . like eating, but not really chewing and swallowing . . . just licking and tasting. "Is that you, Aggie?", I asked her. But she never answered, and it was such a light muffled sound, she could have been sucking on a mint. (*Deep breath.*) I told her I really thought we should leave before it got any darker and we got lost, and this time with real anger in her voice, she said . . . NO! And then the nibbling, or kissing . . . or whatever it was . . . got louder. We reached a clearing, the trees dropped away, the moon shone down on Aggie's bent form as clear as day, and then I saw . . . she was holding one of the little skeletons up to her mouth and . . . was licking it, nibbling on it . . . running her tongue over it. I screamed. She dropped the little thing and turned white. The next thing I knew, she was hitting me with her fists, socking me hard all over my body, screaming and crying, "I hate you! I hate you! I HATE YOU!"

KATE SIV. (*Near tears.*) I'm not listening to this.

BILL PLAID. Oh boy, oh boy, oh boy, all artists are *crazy!*

CHLOE TRAPP. Her perceptual gifts are extraordinary!

BILL PLAID. NUTS! ALL OF THEM!

KATE SIV. You made it up. You made it all up! That didn't happen! NONE OF IT . . . HAPPENED!

BILL PLAID. YOU HAVE TO BE NUTS TO MAKE THE STUFF!

TINK SOLHEIM. (*Puts the sculpture back on its pedestal.*) Agnes Vaag's breath reeks!

THE GUARD. Thank you very much.

TINK SOLHEIM. Her breath is . . . foul!

KATE SIV. You made it up! You've never been invited on one of her expeditions, and you know it. It's your jealousy, Tink . . . your relentless jealousy . . . and it's hateful . . . hateful . . . hateful. . . . (*She runs from the room, sobbing.*)

TINK SOLHEIM. (*Giddy.*) I always noticed a certain animal quality about her breath, a certain . . . rancidness . . . something sour. You know how certain people have breath that doesn't smell quite . . . human?

CHLOE TRAPP. (*Shattered.*) It was at my insistence that Agnes Vaag was invited to exhibit in the show. (*She exits.*)

THE GUARD. For a minute there, you had me worried.

LILLIAN, HARRIET, and MAY. (*Three laughing ladies enter. Their arms are linked and they're on the verge of a belly laugh.* HARRIET *and* MAY *have their eyes covered with their hands as* LILLIAN *leads them to the Moes.*)

LILLIAN. Will you look at that?

HARRIET and MAY. (*Uncover their eyes and look, and let out a piercing shriek of laughter.*)

LILLIAN. (*Also laughing.*) Modern art!

HARRIET and MAY. (*Clutching one another.*) I don't believe it . . . stop . . . oh stop . . . please . . .

LILLIAN. (*Advances to the first Moe and reads the title.*) "Landscape I, 197 , Acrylic emulsion and wax on canvas. On loan from the Sidney Rubin Gallery."
(*All three roar.*)

BILL PLAID. . . . AND YOU HAVE TO BE NUTS TO LOOK AT IT! (*Rises to exit.*) Sucking on statues. . . . I mean, normal people don't go around sucking statues, do they? (*Going up to* THE GUARD.) I've never seen a *normal* person sucking on a statue, have you? First of all, a *normal* person would never even *think* of sucking on a . . .

THE GUARD. (*Gently lays his hands on him.*) Allright, that's enough, quiet down, it's all right. . . . (*Leads him off.*)

BILL PLAID. (*Resisting.*) HEY, WHAT ARE YOU DOING? WHAT ARE YOU THROWING *ME* OUT FOR? I DIDN'T DO ANYTHING . . .(*Pointing to the laughing ladies.*) They're the ones you ought to throw out . . . sucking on statues, Jesus! (*And he's gone.*)

HARRIET. (*Looking at the Moe's.*) There's . . . nothing on them!

MAY. They're . . . blank!

HARRIET. BLANK!

(*All three go off into a shower of laughter again, falling against each other, crossing their legs so they don't wet their pants.*)

LILLIAN. "Landscape II, 197 . Acrylic emulsion and wax on canvas. On loan from the Sidney Rubin Gallery!"

HARRIET. It looks just like the first one.

MAY. Blank!

LILLIAN. No, I like the first one better!

HARRIET. Me too, the first one's better!

(*All three go off into gales.*)

THE GUARD. I just wish this day would end.

LILLIAN. (*At "Starscape 19."*) Now . . . *this* is really special!

HARRIET. You're right, this one's the best!

(*They all stand in front of it.*)

LILLIAN. Guess what the title is?

HARRIET. (*Taking her time.*) Let's see . . . SNOW STORM!

(*All three laugh like crazy.*)

LILLIAN. "Starscape 19!"

HARRIET. I don't see any stars!

LILLIAN. I don't see any paint!

(*All three laugh like crazy again.*)

LILLIAN. (*Reading the title.*) "Acrylic emulsion and wax on canvas." They're all acrylic emulsion and wax.

HARRIET. It must be the latest thing.

LILLIAN. I guess they melt the wax right into the acrylic emulsion.

MAY. What is *acrylic emulsion* anyway?

HARRIET. If you ask me, he should have put a wick in with the wax, and lit a match!

(*All three howl.*)

THE GUARD. Ladies, please. You're disturbing the other visitors in the gallery.

(*It's true, at each outbreak of hysteria, the other people in the room are jolted out of their concentration and look at them with annoyance.*)

LILLIAN, HARRIET, and MAY. (*Work themselves down to the clothesline. They spot GILDA NORRIS on*

the way, furiously sketching from the Moe. They point
at her, then at the Moe and collapse with a fresh
shower of giggles.)

LILLIAN. (*Catches sight of the clothesline, lets out*
her loudest shriek of all.) OH NO!

MAY. (*Diving for the basket, enthralled.*) LOOK AT
THIS, HE LEFT OUT THE BASKET OF
CLOTHESPINS!

THE GUARD. (*Strides over to them.*) Please don't
handle the art works!

MAY. (*Picks up a clothespin.*) Wait a minute, they
don't make this kind of round headed clothespin
anymore.

LILLIAN. (*Takes it from her.*) Let me see. . . .

HARRIET. (*Also taking one.*) I HAVEN'T SEEN
A ROUND HEADED CLOTHESPIN WITHOUT
A SPRING FOR YEARS!

MAY. My mother used to use round headed clothespins like these. I still remember her holding a clothespin just like this and leaning down to show it to me
saying, "Masie, line dried wash hung with round
headed clothespins always hangs better, and don't
you ever forget it!"

LILLIAN. I didn't think they made them anymore.

HARRIET. They must be old. . . .

MAY. The round headed ones grip much better than
the flat headed ones.

LILLIAN. They do, they do!

THE GUARD. (*Trying to get them to put the pins*
back.) Ladies . . . *please!*

MAY. Also, the flat headed ones tend to split in two.

HARRIET. The springs always rusted on the flat
headed ones.

MAY. That's right, and then they'd come shooting
off the line like little rockets. . . .

TINK SOLHEIM. (*Has been gazing at one of the Vaag's. To* THE GUARD *with feeling.*) EACH OF HER PIECES IS A SMALL MIRACLE!

THE GUARD. (*Moves to her, trying to keep an eye on the ladies.*) I know, I know. . . .

TINK SOLHEIM. NO YOU DON'T KNOW! NO-BODY KNOWS!

LILLIAN, HARRIET, and MAY. (*Stealthfully begin to stuff clothespins into their handbags and pockets now that* THE GUARD'S *busy with* TINK. *They try very hard but unsuccessfully to muffle their giggles.*)

THE GUARD. (*To* TINK.) Calm down. . . .

TINK SOLHEIM. There's a secret. . . .

THE GUARD. Yes, Miss, I believe you.

TINK SOLHEIM. Aggie told me that she hid a special surprise inside each piece. . . .

THE GUARD. Yes, I'm sure. . . .

TINK SOLHEIM. It's not visible to the naked eye. You can only find it through vibrations of sound or touch. . . . (*Laying her hands on the lucite dome.*)

THE GUARD. Everything's going to be all right. . . .

TINK SOLHEIM. (*Her movements increasingly manic*). THAT'S THE THING ABOUT AGNES VAAG. SHE ALWAYS TAKES YOU BY SUR-PRISE!

LILLIAN, HARRIET, and MAY. (*Awash with suppressed laughter.*)

THE GUARD. (*Torn in his duty.*) Ladies . . . *please!*

TINK SOLHEIM. She only reveals the surface.

LILLIAN. I've got 12. How many do you have?

HARRIET. (*Giggles.*)

MAY. I've got 7.

LILLIAN. Only 7? Take more.

HARRIET. (*Ecstatic.*) I HAVEN'T SEEN A

ROUND HEADED CLOTHESPIN WITHOUT A
SPRING . . . IN YEARS!

TINK SOLHEIM. She challenged me; FIND THE
MIRACLE, TINK! FIND IT ON THE LAST
DAY!

THE GUARD. (*Dashes over to the ladies.*) LADIES,
LADIES, LADIES! NOW THAT'S ENOUGH.
LET'S PUT ALL THE CLOTHESPINS BACK
LIKE GOOD GIRLS AND TRY AND REMEM-
BER THAT YOU'RE IN A MUSEUM! PUT
THEM BACK IN THE BASKET. . . . EVERY
ONE. HURRY UP. . . . DO AS I SAY. . . .
THAT'S IT . . . THAT'S THE WAY. . . .

LILLIAN, HARRIET, and MAY. (*Leaking clothespins
from their pockets, lurch out of the room, wobbling
with laughter. It's the best time they've had in their
lives.*)

(*It's very quiet. Nothing happens for some time.*)

THE GUARD. (*Out of nowhere sings a long rather
mournful note.*)

LIZ. (*Worn out from her search, enters depressed.*)
Carol? Blakey? Guys? . . . Crud! (*She exits.*)

TINK SOLHEIM. Aggie told me she hid a special
surprise in each piece. She challenged me, find it on
the last day.

THE GUARD. (*Dimly.*) . . . Last day. . . .

GIORGIO and ZOE. (*Enter, a polished couple in their
40's.*)

GIORGIO. Today's the last day. . . .

ZOE. The last day?

TINK SOLHEIM. The last day. . . .

ZOE. I didn't realize it was the last day!

THE GUARD. God in heaven. . . .

GIORGIO. Today's the last day!

TINK SOLHEIM. Laaaaaaaaaaaaast day!

JULIE JENKINS. (*Another photographer enters. A tall, leggy knockout. She carries three times more photographic equipment than the others. She slings it all down in front of the Clothesline.*)

THE GUARD. (*Advancing to her.*) NOW WAIT JUST ONE MINUTE, IT'S AGAINST MUSEUM REGULATIONS TO PHOTOGRAPH THE ART WORKS!

GIORGIO. (*Looking at "Landscape I."*) Zachery Moe!

ZOE. (*To* GIORGIO.) Look at that girl, (TINK.) she's touching one of the statues. . . .

JULIE JENKINS. But today's the last day!

ZOE. Giorgio, look!

THE GUARD. I'm sorry, miss, It's against museum regulations.

GIORGIO. His parents are deaf, I believe.

JULIE JENKINS. But I came to photograph Bill Steven's clothesline!

THE GUARD. You mean, Steve Williams, not Bill Stevens.

JULIE JENKINS. Steve Stevens?

THE GUARD. STEVE WILLIAMS!

JULIE JENKINS. I thought his name was Bill Stevens.

THE GUARD. Steve Stevens?

JULIE JENKINS. (*Desperate.*) WILLIAM STEVENSON!

THE GUARD. Stevenson?

JULIE JENKINS. Williamson?

THE GUARD. Stephen Williamson?

JULIE JENKINS. *WILLIAM* WILLIAMSON!

THE GUARD. Steve!

JULIE JENKINS (*Amazed.*) STEVE?

THE GUARD. Williams!

JULIE JENKINS. *Williams?*

THE GUARD. Steve. Williams!

JULIE JENKINS. Artists always have such tricky names. . . .

GIORGIO. Or is it Raoul Io's parents who are deaf?

ZOE. (*Absorbed with* TINK.) She's not supposed to be doing that.

THE GUARD. You have to get permission from the Director to photograph the art work!

JULIE JENKINS. (*Waving a slip.*) I have permission.

THE GUARD. (*Taking it.*) Yes, I see.

JULIE JENKINS. From the Director. . . .

THE GUARD. Oh?

JULIE JENKINS. Daddy!

ZOE. She's going to get into trouble. . . .

JULIE JENKINS. (*Unloading her gear.*) Daddy's the Director!

ZOE. Look at her, Giorgio!

GIORGIO. (*Examining "Landscape I" up close.*) Very interesting!

JULIE JENKINS. GOD, I LOVE STEVE STEVEN'S WORK!

THE GUARD. The Director's daughter (*Indicating* GILDA NORRIS.) . . . your sister's here too!

ZOE. She's touching them. . . .

GIORGIO. Brilliant brush work!

JULIE JENKINS. All my life I've wanted to photograph a real Bill Stevenson!

GIORGIO. (*Nose against the canvas.*) It's extraordinary how much of the detail you miss when you don't take the time to really examine a canvas!

THE GUARD. (*Going over to him.*) Please sir, don't smell the painting!

GIORGIO. I'm not smelling the painting, I'm examining the brush work!

THE GUARD. Zachery Moe doesn't use a brush!

ZOE. Oh Giorgio!

GIORGIO. He use a roller?

THE GUARD. Nope.

ZOE. Come on, don't start this again.

GIORGIO. Stain technique?

THE GUARD. Nope!

GIORGIO. Spilling?

THE GUARD. No.

(THE GUARD *and* GIORGIO *faster and faster.*)

GIORGIO. Pooling?

THE GUARD. No.

GIORGIO. Scumbling?

THE GUARD. No.

ZOE. People are staring. . . .

GIORGIO. Blotting?

THE GUARD. No.

GIORGIO. Toweling?

THE GUARD. No.

GIORGIO. Shit!

THE GUARD. No.

GIORGIO. AIR BRUSH?

THE GUARD. You got it!

GIORGIO. (*Laughing.*) I knew it all along!

ZOE. Did not. . . .

GIORGIO. (*To* THE GUARD.) In air brushing successive layers of paint, Moe stresses the actuality of the surface and limits the distances between the . . .

ZOE. (*Pulling at him.*) Come on, Giorgio, I'm bored. Let's look at something else. . . . I'm tired of this. . . . come on, let's go to another floor . . . Giorgio!

GIORGIO. (*To* THE GUARD.) It's the relationship of

the figure to the support and the consequent affirmation of the picture plane that makes it difficult to penetrate the atmospheric space behind it . . .

TINK SOLHEIM. (*Suddenly releases the miracle buried in "The Holy Wars of Babylon Rage Through the Night." The lights dim. A floodlight pours down on the statue and Bach's Dorian Toccata and Fugue in D minor, BWV 538 for organ swells from a speaker concealed in the pedestal.*) I FOUND IT! I FOUND IT! "The Holy Wars of Babylon Rage Through the Night!"

EVERYONE. (*Is thunderstruck. They gaze at* TINK *and the statue, chills racing up their backs. There's a hush and slow awakening that the music is* part *of the statue.*)

TINK SOLHEIM. I found the switch. I found it!

GIORGIO. How beautiful. . . .

ZOE. Oh Giorgio. . . .

GILDA NORRIS. I'm going to die. . . .

EVERYONE. (*Slowly draws near the statue to worship.*)

JULIE JENKINS. It's a wave . . . cresting!

GIORGIO. It's a stunning Renaissance landscape. . . .

MICHAEL WALL. It's the urban vision of a futurist.

FRED IZUMI. (*Recites some Haiku in Japanese.*)

GILDA NORRIS. "And lo, the angel of the Lord came upon them, and the glory of the Lord shone around about them . . ."

TINK SOLHEIM. She challenged me: Find it on the last day. . . .

THE GUARD. It's a self portrait.

ZOE. Growth!

(*As the music pours from its source, each viewer improvises the unique beauty he sees. Their voices*

*frequently overlap, but rich details of observation
come through. Private visions are revealed, no one
intrudes on anyone else. This lasts for several
minutes. The volume of the music lowers.)*

TINK SOLHEIM. It was worth it. . . .

ZOE. Nothing like this has ever happened to me
before. . . .

TINK SOLHEIM. It was all worth it . . . *everything!*

THE GUARD. The museum had no idea . . .

GIORGIO. Of course there are precedents for *heard*
art. . . .

ZOE. Giorgio, hold me . . . !

GILDA NORRIS. I'll never forget this day . . . never!

FRED IZUMI. She must have snuck in after the in-
stallation of the show and set it all up. . . .

THE GUARD. None of the security force was told.

TINK SOLHEIM. *She is vindicated!* Through me!
Through me! (*She exits.*)

EVERYONE. (*Takes one last look at the statue and
then drifts to other Agnes Vaag works in hopes of find-
ing their secrets.*)

THE GUARD. (*Watches over "The Holy Wars," trying to figure out what triggered the music and lights.
He breathes on it in a certain way and the music
stops; the lights go back to normal. Baffled, he keeps
circling it.*)

FIRST GUARD. (*Dressed just like* THE GUARD *enters
and joins him.*) Busy?

THE GUARD. (*Caught actually studying part of
the exhibition is embarrassed and feigns indifference.
He whistles.*)

FIRST GUARD. You look busy.

THE GUARD. This is the last day of my show.

FIRST GUARD. Oh, a closing.

SECOND GUARD. (*Dressed as the others, joins them.*) Busy?

THE GUARD. Boy!

FIRST GUARD. I've been swamped!

SECOND GUARD. Colonial Quilts and Weathervanes are slow. I only had three people this morning.

FIRST GUARD. I must have sold $150 worth of postcards in the last hour.

THE GUARD. It's been very busy here.

SECOND GUARD. My show still has two more weeks. I don't know how I'm going to make it, it's so slow.

FIRST GUARD. Engagement calendars aren't doing well, but they just can't get enough postcards!

SECOND GUARD. Very slow.

THE GUARD. The Director has given three photographers permission to photograph the art works.

FIRST and SECOND GUARDS. THREE?

THE GUARD. . . . and a sketcher!

FIRST GUARD. Jesus. . . .

SECOND GUARD. Son of a bitch. . . .

THE GUARD. I don't know where it will end.

FIRST GUARD. (*To the* SECOND GUARD.) You busy this morning? I'm swamped!

SECOND GUARD. Very slow. Only three people. (*Looking around.*) You look pretty busy.

THE GUARD. This is the last day of my show.

SECOND GUARD. I haven't been busy like this since my American Abstract Show last spring.

THE GUARD. They keep stealing my clothespins.

FIRST GUARD. I've just about sold out of your catalogues.

THE GUARD. I'm not surprised.

SECOND GUARD. Thursdays are slow.

FIRST GUARD. Thursdays are slow. But *Tuesdays* . . .

SECOND GUARD. Tuesdays! (*Silence.*) Saturdays are pretty bad.

FIRST GUARD. I'd rather work on a Saturday than a Sunday, though.

SECOND GUARD. Sundays aren't so bad.

THE GUARD. I don't mind Sundays.

SECOND GUARD. I like Sundays.

THE GUARD. Sundays are nice. . . .   SECOND GUARD. Sunday's a good day.

(*Silence.*)

THE GUARD. I just wish people would stop stealing the clothespins.

FIRST GUARD. Hey, did you hear the radio this morning?

SECOND GUARD. THOSE EUROPEAN MUSEUMS HAVE SHIT FOR SECURITY!

(*Everyone looks up.*)

SECOND GUARD. (*Lowering his voice.*) Any maniac can get away with anything in a European museum. Look what happened to Michaelangelo's *Pieta* . . .

FIRST GUARD. And that Rembrandt last year, slashed with a bread knife.

SECOND GUARD. That's right. It could never happen here.

FIRST GUARD. American security is the best.

THE GUARD. You can't beat American security.

FIRST GUARD. NUMBER ONE!

SECOND GUARD. That's right. WE'RE NUMBER ONE ON SECURITY!

(*Everyone looks up again.*)

FIRST GUARD. First!

THE GUARD. The best!

FIRST GUARD. American museums have the tightest security of any museums in the whole fucking world!

THE GUARD and the SECOND GUARD. Yeah you said it, that's right, number one. The best. (etc.)

FIRST GUARD. The people over there are nuts!

THE GUARD and the SECOND GUARD. You can say that again. Here, here. You ain't just whistling "Dixie," (etc.)

FIRST GUARD. Violent bastards. An American would never shoot a painting!

SECOND GUARD. Well, they know they can get away with it over there, so that just encourages them to be violent.

THE GUARD. That's right, that's right!

FIRST GUARD. The worst that's happened over here is some nut with a can of spray paint that washes right off.

SECOND GUARD. Everyone's nuts these days.

THE GUARD. I just wish they'd stop stealing the clothespins!

FIRST GUARD. Did you hear what the guy kept screaming as he shot the painting? "Cursed is the ground for thy sake."

SECOND GUARD. "Cursed is the *ground* for thy sake?"

THE GUARD. Crazy bastards!

FIRST GUARD. It's what Adam said to Eve after she ate the apple.

SECOND GUARD. Jesus.

THE GUARD. Crazy bastards!

FIRST GUARD. Crazy fuckers always yell out something religious when they attack art works!

SECOND GUARD. You wouldn't find me working over there for shit!

FIRST GUARD. They're all nuts on religion over there. . . .

THE GUARD. Crazy bastards. . . .

FIRST GUARD. He pumped 18 bullets into the damned painting before he was restrained. . . . *18 bullets!*
(*Silence.*)

SECOND GUARD. (*Reaches in his pocket.*) Hey, look what I found this morning. Someone must have dropped it.

THE GUARD. Let's see.

FIRST GUARD. What is it?

SECOND GUARD. (*Holding it up to the light.*) A piece of rose quartz.

THE GUARD. (*Takes it and holds it up to the light.*) It looks more like pink tourmaline to me. (*Hands it to the* FIRST GUARD.)

FIRST GUARD. (*Looking at it.*) This isn't tourmaline, it's rhodochorosite!

SECOND GUARD. (*Snatching it back.*) Rhodochrosite shit, it's rose quartz!

FIRST GUARD. It's too opaque to be rose quartz.

THE GUARD. But it's too dense to be rhodochrosite!

SECOND GUARD. Dense? This isn't dense! It's translucent!

FIRST GUARD. (*Holding it up to the light.*) There *are* semi-translucent varieties of rhodochrosite!

THE GUARD. Pink tourmaline can be dense or translucent. It's pink tourmaline.

SECOND GUARD. This can't be pink tourmaline because tourmaline doesn't come in pink!

FIRST GUARD. How could it be rose quartz? It's closer to pink tourmaline . . . even if there's no such animal.

THE GUARD. Rhodochrosite is worth alot more than rose quartz.

FIRST GUARD. . . . or pink tourmaline, for that matter.

SECOND GUARD. (*Putting the stone back in his pocket and pulling out some papers.*) Alright you guys, I've got our assignments for lunch hour.
(*The other guards groan.*)

SECOND GUARD. It's not too bad. (*To* THE GUARD.) Since Lou and George were let go last week, you'll be needed at the register in the Gift Shop because he's (*The* FIRST GUARD.) got to relieve Otto in the Member's Lounge.

THE GUARD. Son of a . . .

SECOND GUARD. (*To the* FIRST GUARD.) You go to the Member's Lounge while I cover for Raoul in the check room since no one's been in the Klein Retrospective all week. Colonial Quilts and Weathervanes is closed for the rest of the day.

THE GUARD. (*In an urgent whisper.*) But someone has to stay here. It's the last day of the show.

SECOND GUARD. You'll be back in a half hour. I just need you to cover for him in the Gift Shop so he can relieve Otto.

THE GUARD. I don't think it's a good idea to leave the room . . . unattended . . .

(*Everyone looks up and then quickly away.*)

SECOND GUARD. It's orders.

THE GUARD. You know what closings are like. Everyone takes things. . . .
(*Everyone looks up again.*)

SECOND GUARD. You mean . . . (*Laughs.*) clothespins? . . .

THE GUARD. Yes, clothespins!

SECOND GUARD. (*Bursts out laughing.*)

FIRST GUARD. (*Joins him.*) *Clothespins!*

THE GUARD. (*Picks up a clothespin to show them.*) They can't get enough of them. They're the old fashioned kind with round heads.

FIRST GUARD. (*Takes it.*) You mean the ones without the spring in the middle?

THE GUARD. That's right.

FIRST GUARD. Jeez, we used to have those. . . .

STEVE WILLIAMS. (*The artist, enters. He radiates charisma. Everyone stares at him; they're not sure who he is, but they know he's someone important and draw back silently. He's come to look at his Clothesline and wears the identical clothes as his self portrait which hangs on the line. He studies the arrangement of the figures from across the room, perplexed.*)

(*A silence.*)

SECOND GUARD. (*Eyes glued to* STEVE WILLIAMS.) You know, I thought my American Abstract Show was busy, but I've got to hand it to you, your's is busier!

THE GUARD. (*Also staring at* WILLIAMS.) Huh?! Huh?!

FIRST GUARD. Come on, we've got to get out of here quietly so no one will notice . . .

THE GUARD. That's right, just slip right out. . . .

SECOND GUARD. Sssssshhhhhhh . . .

(*They exit on tip toe.*)

FIRST GUARD. Listen, the Gift Shop isn't as bad as the Member's Lounge, I don't

THE GUARD. Christ, I hate the Gift Shop! The worst shift of all has got to be the God-

SECOND GUARD. Otto hasn't had lunch for three weeks now, three weeks. His

care what you damned Gift doctor says he's
say. . . . Shop . . . developing in-
(*Etc.*) (*Etc.*) cipent ulcers
 . . . (*Etc.*)

GILDA NORRIS. (*The first to realize, her heart in her throat.*) That's . . . Steve Williams!

GIORGIO. My God, the artist!

ZOE. Oh, Giorgio!

MICHAEL WALL. I thought he looked familiar!

FRED IZUMI. Steve Williams!

ZOE. He's dressed just like° his self portrait!

GILDA NORRIS. (*Swooning.*) Steve . . . Williams?

JULIE JENKINS. STEVE STEVENS!

(*The three photographers quickly take advantage of this media event, and start snapping pictures of* WILLIAMS *and his amazing performance. At times they work independently, and then suddenly strike poses in luscious groupings.*)

STEVE WILLIAMS. (*Ignores everyone and stands engrossed before his work. Something's wrong, the figures aren't positioned correctly. One by one, he unpins the bodies, laying them carefully on the benches and floor until the clothesline is bare. After careful thought he picks up the Mexican boy, cradles him in his arms, and hangs him first on the line. With considerable dash he adds the bride. The third figure to be resurrected is his own which he handles with rough good humor . . . and so on until the lineup is complete. He doesn't make a sound and wields the bodies with such tenderness and ease that everyone is deeply affected.*)

GIORGIO. (*Strides over to the clothesline, his catalogue open, and to heighten the intensity of the moment, reads about* WILLIAMS' *life.*) "Steve Williams was born October 30, 1936, in Santa Rosa, California. He studied at the Leonardo da Vinci School and had his first one man show at the Dilexi Gallery, San Francisco, in 1947, an exhibition of animal heads in cement, which in their open framework and pitted surfaces, were a powerful refutation of the prevailing modern traditions of neat forms, clean surfaces, and truth to materials. Williams lived in Paris from 1947 through 1953 where he exhibited in a group show at the Galerie Maeght, visited Giacometti's studio, and was exposed to and impressed by the works of Paul Klee, Dada, and Surrealism. His sculpture thereafter presented anguished images of the anonymity of modern man, using cast-off objects assembled according to an indisputably human framework. Since 1965, Williams' sculpture, although still governed by the principles of assemblage, comprise more simply structured monumental components, incorporated with technological precision into quite different icons of modernity."

STEVE WILLIAMS. (*Finished with his works, stands back to survey the new lineup. He smiles.*)

(EVERYONE *smiles.*)

THE PHOTOGRAPHERS. (*Pull out all their stops.* JULIE JENKINS *starts using a flash,* MICHAEL WALL *practically stands inside* WILLIAMS' *clothing,* FRED IZUMI *photographs from daring new angles.*)

THE WOMEN IN THE ROOM. (*Reach out their hands towards* WILLIAMS.)

STEVE WILLIAMS. (*Is pleased and walks energetically out of the room, flashing one final smile of goodbye.*)

(*A silence. These lines should spill over each other.*)

GILDA NORRIS. I thought I was going to die . . . just

sink down to the floor, shut my eyes, and quietly die. . . .

JULIE JENKINS. Did you see those hands?

MICHAEL WALL. That was pure . . . once in a life-time!

FRED IZUMI. Harrison isn't going to believe this!

JULIE JENKINS. . . . and his arms. . . . MY GOD, THE TENDERNESS IN HIS ARMS!

GILDA NORRIS. I'll never be the same.

ZOE. But you're not supposed to touch anything once it's been installed, are you?

GIORGIO. His pieces sell for over $200,000! $200,000!

EVERYONE. (*Is silent again, they gaze at the clothes-line for some time.*)

ZOE. Oh Giorgio, let's take something . . . as a re-memberance.

JULIE JENKINS. Steve Stevens. . . .

ZOE. One of the clothespins . . . something he touched.

GILDA NORRIS. Something he touched. . . .

JULIE JENKINS. Something he touched. . . .

MICHAEL WALL. A clothespin. . . .

FRED IZUMI. A clothespin . . .

(*But no one moves.*)

ZOE. (*Breaks the spell, moves to the clothesline and brazenly takes a clothespin.*)

(*One by one each person follows, taking one or more pins. It's not a mad scramble, but a holy communion, enacted with quiet reverence. Once the first theft has been tasted, however, they become thirsty for more. The bride's arm is pulled off with an awful rending sound. Everyone flinches, but stands firm. JULIE JENKINS rushes up to the STEVE WILLIAMS figure and throws her arms*)

around him. GILDA NORRIS *edges past her and
kisses his face; his head falls off in her amazed
hands. The others move in for their share: half
of the Mexican boy is removed, the Businessman's
legs are severed, arms, legs, pieces of clothing are
snatched. The lights dim as each one scurries out
with his booty. The clothesline is almost picked
clean. Only a few stray torsos, hands, and veils
are left.)*

MR. and MRS. MOE. (ZACHERY MOE'S *deaf-mute
parents slip in unnoticed during these final moments.
Caring only for their son's work, they go directly to
his paintings and stand before them, radiant with
pride and happiness.)*

THE GUARD. (*Returns from his lunch break, sees
the devestation of the clothesline and is horrified. He
tries to protect the few scraps that remain and then
starts running in terrible confusion. He finally notices
the* MOES.) What happened in here? What's been going
on? The clothesline! Who did this? Look at it . . .
the clothesline. . . . It's been picked apart . . . destroyed . . . what happened? WILL YOU PLEASE
TELL ME . . . WHAT HAPPENED? WHO DID
THIS? (*They don't answer. He realizes they can't
answer in his language. He kneels by the basket of
clothespins, broken.)*

MR. and MRS. MOE. (*Keep gazing at the paintings,
completely unaware of* THE GUARD. MRS. MOE *turns
to her husband and moves her hands in sign language.
He answers her. The lights fade around them as they
stand rooted before their son's work, their hands de-
scribing his youth and great promise.)*

AS THE CURTAIN SLOWLY FALLS

EPILOGUE

*This is what the Moes are saying in sign language:

MRS. MOE. Remember the drawings he used to make as a child?

MR. MOE. The sketches he did of all his toys in his nursery . . .

MRS. MOE. How wonderful they were, bursting with life . . .

MR. MOE. *Noisy* with life!

MRS. MOE. Remember how he'd make the walls shake when he wanted something?

MR. MOE. And how they shook! He shouted with the voice of a thousand men!

PROPERTY LIST

Preset on Stage
   2 large benches
   4 smaller benches
   3 large white canvases
   1 large plexiglass case—with possible 4 sculptures
   6 pedestals with 5 sculptures

   Construction—clothesline with 5 soft figures and drop
   Basket with round headed clothespins
   Museum map in case
   Brochures in case

Hand Props—Off Stage
   Photo equipment (Michael Wall)
   Bilingual catalogue (Jean-Claude)
   Catalogue (Liz)
   Catalogue (Mr. Hollingsford)
   Permission slip (Michael Wall)
   Recorded Tour—2 ear plugs (Mr. Salt)
   Photo equipment (Fred Izumi)
   Recorded tour (Mr. Gregory)
   Permission slip (Fred Izumi)
   Folding chair, sketch book and pencil (Gilda Norris)
   Stained scarf (Kate Siv)
   3 handbags (Lillian, Harriet, May)
   Photo equipment (Julie Jenkins)
   Rose quartz (2nd Guard)
   Assignment papers (2nd Guard)
   Catalogue (Giorgio)
   3 recorded tour units (5 out of towners)

Photo equipment might be any combination of camera bag,
camera, tripod and light meter.

Set Pieces and Stage Preset
   5 Dummies (preset order from Downstage to Upstage)
   business man—Upstage of plexiglass plate; leg tabs preset
      only top ½ inch; handkerchief struck from pocket; check

77

garter; check cigar (hot glue); check Head (velcro front
and back of collar)

Mexican boy—check eyes (hot glue); tabs at waist front
and back; both ½'s of body attached solidly

Bride—veil fluffed and free from spacers (preset over top
line); centered between spacers; check both arms; extra
space allowed on both Downstage and Upstage sides

Chinese girl—hair brushed and preset over bottom line;
check hair not entangled in hooks; Downstage bosom
attached with dark shading at bottom; feet attached with
bows on outside of feet

Artist—head attached with velcro both front and back, check
leg tabs; check Upstage arm tab; check velcro on Upstage
sleeve and sleeve unbuttoned; check pencil struck from
artist ear; check glasses (hot glue)

4 clothespins on bottom line—holding Businessman and Boy

Double clothesline—attached to Down Right corner of
flat and stantion

2 birds—wired on line 1 just Downstage of Downstage spacer;
1 on top of Upstage wheel; check secure and upright

1 stantion—clean bottom

1 backdrop with extra bricks—check bricks secured

1 basket of clothespins—check all round headed; preset
in front of Bride—length Downstage and Upstage; ap-
proximately 5 inches left

2 large benches—center, Upstage and Downstage, check
spikes and clean

2 smaller benches—Down Right and Down Left, in jogs,
check, spikes and clean

3 large white canvases with plexiglass nameplates—polish
plates

1 museum floorplan—polish plexiglass

1 plexiglass brochure case—polish and check brochures

1 hydrometer—polish

1 plexiglass case attached to Upstage Right flat with 3
sculptures—cleaned and polished

3 pedestals with sculpture in each; Upstage Right—clean
base and polish inside and out; Upstage Left—clean base
and polish outside; Downstage Left—clean base and polish
inside and out; wipe inside edge of pedestal

Downstage Right Door—closed, polish plexiglass

Check black tape on floor and paint—retape if necessary

Hand Props—Backstage Center Table
GUARD:
1 keyring with key; 1 white handkerchief
MICHAEL WALL:
1 Nikkon camera with lens cap, without strap preset on;
1 tripod—cranked up 6 inches and tightened; 1 soft black
camera case—preset with: 1 extra lens and cap; 1 photo
journal sheet; 1 pack lens paper; 1 pencil; Preset in outside pocket of case: 1 camera strap—accessible to actor;
2 rolls film; 1 light meter; gum
JEAN-CLAUDE:
*1 catalogue
LIZ:
1 catalogue
MR. HOLLINGSFORD:
1 catalogue; 1 floorplan
MICHAEL WALL:
1 permission slip made out for
FRED IZUMI:
1 permission slip made out for
PETER ZIFF:
1 pencil (medium small); 1 red handkerchief (keeps with
costume)
THE SALTS:
1 acoustiguide—charged, volume set with double notch at
12 o'clock; 1 tape (preset in Salts machine); 2 sets earphones; 1 son- alert unit
MAGGIE SNOW:
1 NYU notebook with pentel in spiral; 1 pr. gold rim
glasses
FRED IZUMI:
1 black hard edge camera bag (preset with: 1 Nikkon camera
with lens and cap; 1 camera strap; 1 light meter; 1 film
can; 1 pentel; 1 brochure
BOB LAMB:
1 channel 13 bag stuffed with 2 T-shirts and 1 catalogue
FIRST MAN IN PASSING:
1 clipboard with legal pad
SECOND MAN IN PASSING:
1 pack of cigarettes; 1 pencil (medium small)

*NOTE: All catalogues have sketches and Giorgio text. These
pages are dog earred. All are identical.

BARBARA CASTLE:

1 tan handbag stuffed and preset in side zip pocket with: 1 compact; 1 nail file; 1 box baby powder; 1 dulled Bendel gift box- rigged with: handle, stuffed lightly with 1 layer foam; 1 Berdorf box—taped and stuffed lightly with 1 layer of foam

BARBARA ZIMMER:

1 brochure; 1 gold pen; 1 catalogue

MR. GREGORY:

1 acoustiguide—I.D. red arrow on side of machine, charged and preset with: 1 Gregory tape—cued up and volume full; 1 set earphones

GUARD:

1 assignment slip; American flag pin on lapel of costume; 1 piece pink quartz

BILL PLAID:

1 blue notebook (small) with: 1 ballpoint pen

HARRIET:

1 brown bag preset with: 1 handkerchief

MAY:

1 handkerchief preset in coat pocket

GIORGIO:

1 catalogue

JULIE JENKINS:

1 brown handbag preset with: (stuffed); 1 extra flash cube inside zipper pocket; 1 instamatic camera preset to wind, with new cube; with at least 4 exposures

STEVE WILLIAMS:

1 leather tote bag (stuffed) preset with: 1 white handkerchief inside zip pocket; 1 pencil—new inside zip pocket; 1 eyeglasses set in costume pocket

GILDA NORRIS:

1 folding stool; 1 large white canvas bag preset with: 2 sketch pads—old sketches removed; colored pencils in one side pocket opposite side pocket preset; 1 pack chalk; 2 conte crayons; 1 white magic marker; 1 sharpened white pencil; 1 gum eraser; 1 pencil sharpener

PROPERTY RUNNING NOTES

1. After Backstage Blackout at top of show:
   A. Reset Barbara handbag and Bergdorf and Bendel boxes Back Stage Left of makeup table Back Stage Left

2. Michael Wall's exit Upstage Left:
    A. Meet and collect tripod
    B. Fold tripod and strike to small roadbox
3. Maggie Snow exit p. 26 Upstage Right:
    A. Meet and collect props and costumes
    B. Return notebook, pen and glasses to prop table
    C. Return sweater, coat and canvas bag to costume rack
       Back Stage Left
    D. Assist with quick change—½ slip and skirt-zip and top
       closure
    E. Clear Maggie Snow costume from quick-change area
       to costume rack
Note: If/when powder is used for "White Rash," powder left
    arm and button sleeve. Floor should be wiped with
    damp cloth to prevent accidents—slipping on powder.
    All Maggie Snow activity must be completed by Liz
    exit p. 28 for Liz/Mira quick change.
4. Jean-Claude exits p. 25 with catalogue:
    A. Actor returns catalogue to prop table before Entrance
       as man-in-passing p. 30
    B. Catalogue may be struck to roadbox
5. Two men-in-passing exit Upstage Right p. 32:
    A. Clipboard returned by actor
    B. Strike Maggie Snow notebook, glasses and clipboard
       to roadbox
6. After p. 32 and before Mr. Gregory entrance p. 41:
    A. Actor returns cigarettes and pencil
    B. Strike to roadbox
7. Salts exit Upstage Left p. 43:
    A. Meet at prop table, untangle and assist with acousti-
       guide
    B. Rewind tape and remove from machine
    C. Coil earphones
    D. Strike earphones tape and son-alert unit to roadbox
    E. Temporarily store acoustiguide on top of roadbox
Note: After performance acoustiguides taken to prop room
    and locked in charging unit.
8. Bob Lamb and Will Willard exit Upstage Left p. 54:
    A. Meet and collect Channel 13 bag from Lamb
    B. Collect catalogue and ring from Willard
    C. Remove clothes pins from bag
    D Strike bag and catalogue to roadbox

9. For Bill Plaid entrance Upstage Left p. 61:
   A. Hand notebook and pen to actor after quick change Back Stage Left Lamb/Plaid
10. Two Barbara's exit p. 56:
    A. Actress returns 2 boxes and handbag to prop table
    B. Collect catalogue from ladies dressing area Back Stage Left
    C. Strike 2 boxes, 1 handbag and 1 catalogue to roadbox
11. Mr. Gregory exits p. 58 Upstage Left:
    See (7) same procedure for acoustiguide
12. Between p. 71 and 75, before Zoe's entrance Upstage Right:
    A. Tie bow of jumper costume and check snaps
13. After p. 70 Bill Plaid exits Upstage Right:
    A. Actor returns notebook and pen
    B. Strike to roadbox
14. Laughing Ladies exit Upstage Left p. 77:
    A. Meet in dressing room Back Stage Right to collect clothes pins—check coat pockets and handbag
    B. Check May's coat for handkerchief, 1 brown handbag with gloves and handkerchief
Note: Handkerchief occasionally dropped on stage—retrieved after performance.
    Handbag struck to roadbox.
15. Peter Zeff exits Down Stage p. 77:
    A. After costume change collect pencils from Back Stage Down Right Men's dressing area
16. After Liz exit Upstage Right p. 77:
    A. 5 catalogues should be struck to roadbox
17. Between p. 77 and p. 87 Before Guards enter:
    A. Check 3rd guard actor who occasionally powders face/beard
    B. Powder can be struck to roadbox after checking with actor
18. Steve Williams entrance Back Stage Left p. 96:
    A. Meet before entrance to collect eyeglass case
19. Guards exit Down Right p. 97:
    A. Meet and collect keys, quartz, clothes pins
    B. Strike to roadbox
20. Steve Williams exits Upstage Left p. 99:
    A. Meet and collect bag and eyeglasses
    B. Return ring
    C. Strike bag and eyeglasses in case to roadbox

21. Body Snatchers exit p. 101—Giorgio, Zoe, Wall, Gilda, and Izumi Upstage Right—Jenkins Upstage Left:

Note: Props have been struck during performance to make room for Dummy parts on prop table—table should be cleared for this exit.

    A. Collect bag, Instamatic and artist arm from Julie Jenkins Back Stage Right

    B. Strike bag to roadbox

    C. Instamatic to small roadbox

22. Collect Wall—Nikkon business man's head and leg Back Stage Left

    A. Head and leg on prop table

    B. Strike Nikkon to small roadbox—all other props and dumy parts are returned to prop table by actors

    C. Collect Izumi camera and lock-up all photo equipment

    D. Remove artist head and leg from Gilda bag

    E. Strike bag and stool to roadbox

23. After Curtain Call:

NOTE—All dummy parts should be on prop table (i.e.—two bride's arms, businessman's head, businessman's leg, Chinese girl bosom, Chinese girl two feet, ½ Mexican boy, artist leg, artist head, artist arm).

    A. Retrieve from stage—catalogue, pencil and handkerchief/handkerchieves and strike to roadbox

    B. Return clothes pins

    C. Check and repair dummies

    D. Reset dummies and hang tarp

    E. Empty water pitchers—ashtrays

    F. Clean up dressing rooms

    G. Take photo equipment to prop room

    H. Take acoustiguides to prop room and charge

PERSONALS Set in Dressing Rooms

BARBARA ZIMMER:
1 catalogue without dogears

HARRIET:
brown handbag with gloves and handkerchief

PROPERTY PRESET OFFSTAGE

handkerchief occasionally dropped on stage.

handkerchief washed by
costumes twice a week
and returned for per-
formances.

MAY:
  handkerchief   kept in costume coat
                                     pocket.

PETER ZIFF:
  red handkerchief   kept in costume pants.
STEVE WILLIAMS:
  eyeglasses in case   preset in shirt pocket.
3RD GUARD:
  gum   one piece of gum preset
                                     inside pocket of jacket.
  American flag pin   check American flag pin on
                                     lapel.

✔✔✔✔✔✔✔✔✔✔✔✔✔✔✔✔✔✔✔✔✔✔✔✔✔✔✔✔✔✔

OTHER PUBLICATIONS FOR YOUR INTEREST

COASTAL DISTURBANCES
(Little Theatre- Comedy)

by TINA HOWE

3 male, 4 female

This new Broadway hit from the author of *PAINTING CHURCHES, MUSEUM,* and *THE ART OF DINING* is quite daring and experimental, in that it is *not* cynical or alienated about love and romance. This is an ensemble play about four generations of vacationers on a Massachusetts beach which focuses on a budding romance between a hunk of a lifeguard and a kooky young photographer. Structured as a series of vignettes taking place over the course of the summer, the play looks at love from all sides now. "A modern play about love that is, for once, actually about love--as opposed to sexual, social or marital politics . . . it generously illuminates the intimate landscape between men and women." --NY Times. "Enchanting."--New Yorker. #5755

APPROACHING ZANZIBAR
(Advanced Groups—Comedy)

by TINA HOWE

2 male, 4 female, 3 children --Various Ints. and Exts.

This new play by the author of *Painting Churches, Coastal Disturbances, Museum,* and *The Art of Dining* is about the cross-country journey of the Blossom family--Wallace and Charlotte and their two kids Turner and Pony--out west to visit Charlotte's aunt Olivia Childs in Taos, New Mexico. Aunt Olivia, a renowned environmental artist who creates enormous "sculptures" of hundreds of kites, is dying of cancer, and Charlotte wants to see her one last time. The family camps out along the way, having various adventures and meeting other relatives and strangers, until, eventually, they arrive in Taos, where Olivia is fading in and out of reality--or is she? Little Pony Blossom persuades the old lady to stand up and jump up and down on the bed, and we are left with final entrancing image of Aunt Olivia and Pony bouncing on the bed like a trampoline. Has a miracle occurred? "What pervades the shadow is Miss Howe's originality and purity of her dramatic imagination."--The New Yorker. #3140

NEW COMEDIES FROM
SAMUEL FRENCH, INC.

MAIDS OF HONOR. (Little Theatre.) Comedy. Joan Casademont. 3m., 4f. Comb Int./Ext. Elizabeth McGovern, Laila Robins and Kyra Sedgwick starred in this warm, wacky comedy at Off-Broadway's famed WPA Theatre. Monica Bowlin, a local TV talk-show host, is getting married. Her two sisters, Isabelle and Annie, are intent on talking her out of it. It seems that Mr. Wonderful, the groom-to-be, is about to be indicted for insider trading, a little secret he has failed to share with his fiancee, Monica. She has a secret she has kept herself, too—she's pregnant, possibly not by her groom-to-be! All this is uncovered by delightfully kookie Isabelle, who aspires to be an investigative reporter. She'd also like to get Monica to realize that she is marrying the wrong man, for the wrong reason. She should be marrying ex-boyfriend Roger Dowling, who has come back to return a diary Monica left behind. And sister Annie should be marrying the caterer for the wedding, old flame Harry Hobson—but for some reason she can't relax enough to see how perfect he is for her. The reason for all three Bowlin women's difficulties with men, the reason why they have always made the wrong choice and failed to see the right one, is that they are the adult children of an alcoholic father and an abused mother, both now passed away, and they cannot allow themselves to love because they themselves feel unlovable. Sound gloomy and depressing? No, indeed. This delightful, wise and warm-hearted new play is loaded with laughs. We would also like to point out to all you actors that the play is also loaded with excellent monologues, at least one of which was recently included in an anthology of monologues from the best new plays.)   (#14961)

GROTESQUE LOVESONGS. (Little Theatre.) Comedy. Don Nigro. (Author of *The Curate Shakespeare As You Like It, Seascape with Sharks and Dancer* and other plays). This quirky new comedy about a family in Terre Haute, Indiana, enchanted audiences at NYC's famed WPA Theatre. Two brothers, Pete and John, live with their parents in a big old house with an attached greenhouse. The father, Dan, has a horticulture business. A pretty young woman named Romy is more or less engaged to marry younger brother Johnny as the play begins, and their prospects look quite rosy, for Johnny has just inherited a ton of money from recently-deceased family friend, Mr. Agajanian. Why, wonders Pete, has Agajanian left his entire estate to Johnny? He starts to persistently ask this question to his mother, Louise. Eventually, Louise does admit that, in fact, Mr. Agajanian was Johnny's father. This news stuns Johnny; but he's not *really* staggered until he goes down to the greenhouse and finds Pete and Romy making love. Pete, it seems, has always desperately wanted Romy; but when she chose Johnny instead he married a woman in the circus who turned out to be a con artist, taking him for everything he had and then disappearing. It seems everyone but Johnny is haunted by a traumatic past experience: Louise by her affair with Agajanian; Dan by the memory of his first true love, a Terre Haute whore; Pete by his failed marriage, and Romy by her *two* failed marriages. (One husband she left; the other was run over by a truckload of chickens [He loved cartoons so much, says Romy, that it was only fitting he should die like Wile E. Coyote.]). And, each character but Johnny knows what he wants. Louise and Dan want the contentment of their marriage; Romy wants to bake bread in a big old house—and she wants Pete, who finally admits that he wants her, too. And, finally, Johnny realizes what he wants. He does not want the money, or Agajanian's house. He wants to go to Nashville to make his own way as a singer of sad—yes, grotesque—love songs in the night. NOTE: this play is a treasure-trove of scene and monologue material.)   (#9925)

ESTABLISHED PRICE
By Dennis McIntyre

(Little Theatre.) Comedy. 4m. Int. This timely new comedy by the author of *Split Second* and *Modigliani* has had two major successful regional productions, and is now available for the first time. It is a comedy of white-collar angst in this age of corporate takeovers, focusing on the predicament of middle-aged managers who suddenly find themselves out of a job—like just above everyone else—when the company for whom they have worked most of their working lives is taken over and dismantled by a corporate raider. True, each is provided with a handsome "golden parachute"—but this is small recompense—as well as an inadequate replacement for—their jobs, which have become their identity. The central character, Frank Daniels (played in Philadelphia by Kenneth McMillan and at the Long Wharf Theatre by Jason Robards) is the former general counsel for the cannibalized corporation—and he does not intend to go gently into the good night of his forced retirement. He refuses to pack, tears up the office, and tries to get his fellow executives to decline their golden parachutes as a protest over what has happened to them. Naturally, they think he's crazy, which he may just be—and they certainly do not intend to give back their checks. In the end, even Frank capitulates, and pockets the check. He may be crazy, but he's not stupid! "Taut and heart-felt."—Phila. Daily News. "Our playwrights are supposed to do this for us. They are supposed to bring into the open whatever it is that is eating away at us, as Arthur Miller once did and as few playwrights have done since. Now comes Dennis McIntyre, locating the trouble and lifting it from the financial pages of our newspaper to put it in the context of our lives. His play about a corporate takeover is a searchlight revealing the latest alarming shift of the national energy away from people and toward the bottom line."—Phila. Inquirer. "[A] knowing and extremely timely new play."—N.Y. Times.. **(#7085)**

NATIONAL ANTHEMS
By Dennis McIntyre

(Little Theatre.) Comic Drama. 2m., 1f. Int. Tom Berenger, Kevin Spacey and Mary McDonnell starred in the acclaimed Long Wharf Theatre production of this insightful, hard-hitting new play from the author of *Modigliani, Split Second* and *Established Price*. We are in the sumptuous home of Arthur and Leslie Reed, who have had a party that evening for their neighbors. It is very late , and all the guests have gone home, when one final guest arrives, a fireman named Ben Cook, a working man not, shall we say, from the Reeds' socio-economic background. Nonetheless, the Reeds play gracious hosts—until, that is, things get nasty, as Ben increasingly shows his desperation about everything his life lacks in the way of material comforts, status and personal pride. Eventually, the two men get drunk as skunks and come to blows, in this apt parable about America's love-affair with materialism. "Topical, perverse and funny."—Variety. "Profane, smart and disturbingly funny . . . with an acuteness that's as up-to-date as this morning's newspaper headlines."—Rochester Times-Union. "Excoriating assault on traditional American values. Mr. McIntyre demonstrates his visceral sense of theatricality as well as his own state-of-the-heart awareness of contemporary behavior."—N.Y. Times. **(#15982)**

THE BABY DANCE
Little Theatre-Drama
by Jane Anderson

3m., 2f. 2 Ints. Stephanie Zimbalist starred in the original production of this brilliant, moving new drama, both at the Pasadena Playhouse and at the Long Wharf Theatre. She played a woman from Los Angeles named Rachel who has everything she wants in life—except a child. Rachel has located a poor couple who have more children than they can afford to keep, and have agreed to let their latest, when it is born, be adopted by Rachel and her husband. Desperate for a healthy baby, Rachel is paying for all of the poor woman's pre-natal care and hospital expenses. When she arrives for a visit at the trailer park where Al and Wanda live, she is appalled to find that Wanda is not eating correctly. She is also appalled by Al, who actually comes on to her when he is not seething with resentment. The whole arrangement nearly falls through, but by the second act, both couples are back on track. Until, that is, it is learned that the newborn baby may—just may—have suffered some brain damage in the difficult birth, causing Wanda's husband to back away from the deal, much to Rachel's chagrin. Rachel wants the baby anyway, wants to take the chance. In the end, the childless couple do renege on the deal, leaving Wanda and Al with yet another mouth to feed. "The best play produced this season at the Long Wharf Theatre and the first in several seasons to touch the heart so profoundly."—New Haven Advocate. "*The Baby Dance* is not just a 'woman's play.' It is a gripping drama that leaves the audience with more empathy for these people than they would have thought possible."—Bridgeport Post. "A powerful, deeply wrenching drama."—Berkshire Eagle. "It would take a heart of stone to be unmoved by Jane Anderson's *The Baby Dance*.".   (#4305)

THE BATTLE OF SHALLOWFORD
Little Theatre-Comedy
by Ed Simpson

8m., 1f. Int. On a quiet Sunday night, the local regulars have gathered at Burton Mock's general store, in the small town of Shallowford, NC. It is October, 1938. The rest of the world is poised on the brink of war, but the locals aren't much worried about events in the world at large. They're more interested in the local gossip—and Burton's general store is the best place to hear it. The regulars include the gossipy, whining Clunette; fey church choirmaster Fred; lowlife, wild-eyed Newsome Jarvis, on hand with his "slow" son, Doodad; Mr. Roy, a one-armed World War I veteran who holds court at the store; egotistic local football hero Dewey Sowers; Burton's restless young daughter, Ruthie; and her schoolmate Lonny Hutchins, a sci-fi aficionado. All is calm; until, that is, they turn on the radio and learn that the Martians have invaded! Of course, it is the famous Orson Welles broadcast they are listening to—but they fall for it hook, line and shotgun, and run out to do battle against the fearsome threat from the invading Martians. Only Lonny suspects that something is fishy, but he's got his hands full if he thinks he's gonna deter the local yokels from their moment of glory. This delightful new comedy has had several successful productions nation-wide, and is finally available to y'all. Read it if you want a good laugh; produce it if that's how you like your audience to respond. "A theatrical gem."—Asheville Citizen-Times. "Tickle their funny bones, warm their hearts, don't insult their intelligence ... Ed Simpson's *The Battle of Shallowford* hits that magic trio."—Knoxville News-Sentinel. "A sentimental comedy that's hilariously on target. It could easily become a community theatre staple in much the way the works of Larry Shue have."—Knoxville Journal. A cassette tape of excerpts from the Mercury Theatre's radio broadcast of "The War of the Worlds" called for in the text of the play is available for $10, plus postage.   (#4315)